Computer Dictionary

VISUAL 3D SERIES

by: maranGraphics' Development Group

Corporate Sales	**Canadian Trade Sales**
Contact maranGraphics Phone: (905) 890-3300, ext.206 　　　　(800) 469-6616, ext.206 Fax:　 (905) 890-9434	Contact Prentice Hall Canada Phone: (416) 293-3621 　　　　(800) 567-3800 Fax:　 (416) 299-2529

Computer Dictionary

Canadian Cataloguing in Publication Data
Graham, Gordon
　　　　　Computer dictionary

(Visual 3-D series)
Includes index.
ISBN 1-896283-13-6

1. Computers - Dictionaries.　2. Electronic data
processing - Dictionaries.　3. IBM computers -
Dictionaries.　I. MaranGraphics Inc.　II. Title.
III. Series.

QA76.15.M373 1995　　　　004'.03　　　　C95-931823-2

Printed in the United States of America

10　9　8　7　6　5　4　3　2　1

Trademark Acknowledgments

The animated characters are the
copyright of maranGraphics, Inc.

Computer Dictionary

·VISUAL 3D SERIES·

maranGraphics™

*Every maranGraphics book represents
the extraordinary vision and commitment of a unique family:
the Maran Family of Toronto, Canada.*

Back Row (from left to right): *Sherry Maran, Rob Maran, mG, Richard Maran, Maxine Maran, Jill Maran.*
Front Row (from left to right): *mG, Judy Maran, Ruth Maran, mG.*

Richard Maran is the company founder and its inspirational leader. He began maranGraphics over twenty years ago with a vision of a more efficient way to communicate a visual grammar that fuses text and graphics and allows readers to instantly grasp concepts.

Ruth Maran is the Author and Architect—a role Richard established that now bears Ruth's distinctive touch. She creates the words and visual structure that are the basis for the books.

Judy Maran is Senior Editor. She works with Ruth, Richard, and the highly talented maranGraphics illustrators, designers, and editors to transform Ruth's material into its final form.

Rob Maran is the Technical and Production Specialist. He makes sure the state-of-the art technology used to create these books always performs as it should.

Sherry Maran manages the Reception, Order Desk, and any number of areas that require immediate attention and a helping hand.

Jill Maran is a jack-of-all-trades and dynamo who fills in anywhere she's needed anytime she's back from university.

Maxine Maran is the Business Manager and family sage. She maintains order in the business and family—and keeps everything running smoothly.

Oh, and there's **mG**. He's maranGraphics' spokesperson and, well, star. When you use a maranGraphics book, you'll see a lot of mG and his friends. They're just part of the family!

Credits

Author:
Gordon Graham

Project Manager:
Judy Maran

Technical Reviewer:
Geof Wheelwright

Internet Consultant:
Neil Mohan

Editors:
Brad Hilderley
Catherine Manson
Ruth Maran
Kelleigh Wing
Paul Lofthouse

Layout Designer:
Christie Van Duin

Illustrations:
Dave Ross
David de Haas
Tamara Poliquin
Chris K.C. Leung
Russ Marini

Post Production:
Robert Maran

Acknowledgments

Thanks to the dedicated staff of maranGraphics, including David de Haas, Brad Hilderley, Chris K.C. Leung, Paul Lofthouse, Catherine Manson, Jill Maran, Judy Maran, Maxine Maran, Robert Maran, Ruth Maran, Sherry Maran, Russ Marini, Neil Mohan, Tamara Poliquin, Dave Ross, Andrew Trowbridge, Christie Van Duin, and Kelleigh Wing.

Finally, to Richard Maran who originated the easy-to-use graphic format of this guide. Thank you for your inspiration and guidance.

This book shows and tells you what all those computer terms really mean!

The header on each 2-page spread displays the terms covered.

OCR – Operating System

OCR (OPTICAL CHARACTER RECOGNITION)

Software that can read handwritten or printed text. OCR software interprets the lines and squiggles on a page and converts them into characters. This provides a quick way to enter text into your computer. OCR software is commonly used with scanners.

OFF-SITE STORAGE

Storing a copy of important files in a separate location. This provides an extra copy of your files just in case your house burns down or your computer is stolen.

WHAT'S IN THIS BOOK?

This book covers the most common computer terms you're likely to encounter when reading about hardware, software, multimedia, and the Internet.

You won't find any high-tech jargon or technobabble: all terms are explained with simple words and full-color illustrations.

ONLINE

Plugged in and ready for action. Online describes two devices connected by a telephone or computer cable that are ready and able to communicate. For example, your computer is online when you dial another computer with your modem and make a connection.

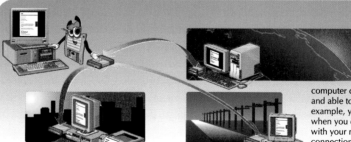

128

At the front of the book, you will find numbers like 486 and 24-bit.

BOOK WORKS

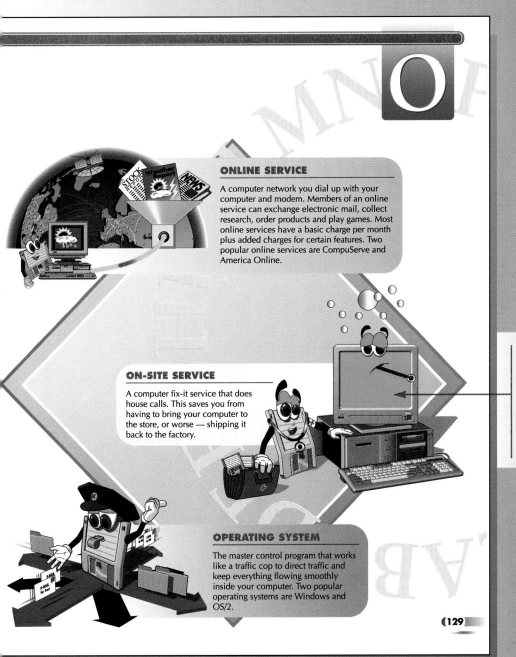

ONLINE SERVICE

A computer network you dial up with your computer and modem. Members of an online service can exchange electronic mail, collect research, order products and play games. Most online services have a basic charge per month plus added charges for certain features. Two popular online services are CompuServe and America Online.

ON-SITE SERVICE

A computer fix-it service that does house calls. This saves you from having to bring your computer to the store, or worse — shipping it back to the factory.

OPERATING SYSTEM

The master control program that works like a traffic cop to direct traffic and keep everything flowing smoothly inside your computer. Two popular operating systems are Windows and OS/2.

On each 2-page spread, the text and graphics for each term are visually integrated using our award-winning communication technology. The result is a book that is both entertaining and as accurate as a technical manual.

At the back of the book, two indexes are included:
1) for popular acronyms like FAQ and PCI,
2) for Internet terms.

4-Bit Color – 24-Bit Color

The number of colors a monitor can display determines how realistic images will appear on your screen. More colors result in more realistic images.

4-BIT COLOR (16 COLORS)

You can use 16 colors for office work like word processing, but not for displaying graphics. With only 16 colors, there is too much of a jump from one color to the next, so obvious "bands" of color appear.

8-BIT COLOR (256 COLORS)

This is good for most home and business uses, and a good balance between screen quality and price. Some "bands" of color are still visible, which undermine the realism of the images. You need at least 256 colors for multimedia.

16-BIT COLOR (65,536 COLORS)

This is good for desktop publishing and advanced multimedia, when you want to see realistic photos and videos. All the colors blend into one another to yield high-quality images.

The greater the number of colors your monitor displays, the slower your computer runs and the more memory you need on your video card.

24-BIT COLOR (16.7 MILLION COLORS)

Also called "true color", this displays high-quality photographs and videos. It is used mainly by professional designers and computer artists for retouching digital photos.

386 Chip –
32-Bit Operating System

386 CHIP

An older CPU chip that is no longer sold in new machines. 386 chips run much slower than 486 chips, and aren't powerful enough for multimedia.

486 CHIP

A more recent CPU chip that is being replaced by the newer Pentium chips. Many computers still use the 486, which offers excellent value and performance for word processing and other office work. You need at least a 486 for multimedia.

586 (OR PENTIUM) CHIP

A powerful CPU chip. Called "Pentium" by Intel, 586 is a generic name used by other manufacturers. The Pentium (or 586) chip is twice as fast as the 486 chip and is preferred for Windows computers due to its high speed and performance.

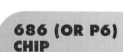

686 (OR P6) CHIP

The most powerful CPU chip (code named P6 by Intel). The P6 (or 686) chip is twice as fast as the Pentium chip. Of course, this makes it more expensive.

8-BIT AND 16-BIT SOUND

This number measures the quality of a sound card: the more bits, the better the sound. Older 8-bit sound cards produce so-so sound; don't buy one even if you can still find one. Newer 16-bit sound cards produce high-fidelity sound and music, making them the standard for multimedia.

16-BIT AND 32-BIT OPERATING SYSTEM

The operating system is the master control program that keeps everything flowing smoothly inside your computer. Older operating systems could only deal with 16 bits of information at once. Newer operating systems can handle 32 bits, which means they do more in less time. Microsoft's Windows 95 and IBM's OS/2 Warp are two popular 32-bit operating systems.

There are four types of 486 chips.

486SX
486DX
486DX2
486DX4

486SX

An SX chip does not have a built-in math coprocessor.

486DX

A DX chip is the same as an SX chip, except it has a built-in math coprocessor. This makes a DX chip more expensive but faster at performing complex math calculations.

Math coprocessor

A math coprocessor assists the CPU by performing complex mathematical calculations. It can speed up your computer when you are working with graphics, scientific applications or math-intensive spreadsheets.

A math coprocessor is also called a floating point coprocessor or floating point unit.

486DX2

A DX2 chip also has a built-in math coprocessor but processes and calculates information twice as fast as a DX chip. This improves the overall computer performance by up to 1.7 times.

486DX4

A DX4 chip also has a built-in math coprocessor but processes and calculates information three times as fast as a DX chip. This improves the overall computer performance by up to 2.5 times.

Absolute Reference – Active Cell

ABSOLUTE REFERENCE

Naming a cell in a spreadsheet with dollar signs (example A14), to point to a fixed number you often use, like a sales tax rate. An absolute reference is "locked in" so it doesn't change, even if you copy your formula to a different cell. See also RELATIVE REFERENCE.

ACCELERATOR CARD

A special expansion card you can add to your computer to make it faster. For example, a graphics accelerator card reduces the time it takes the computer to display images on your screen.

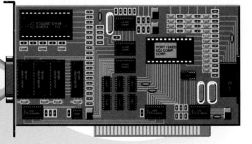

ACCESS PRIVILEGES

What you need to log on to most computer networks. Having access privileges means you have an account and a password that let you use a network.

As you enter your password, it appears as a line of ******** to protect it from prying eyes.

ACCESS PROVIDER

See SERVICE PROVIDER.

ACCESS TIME

How long it takes to find information on a hard disk or CD-ROM. Access time is given in thousandths of a second (milliseconds). The lower the access time, the faster the drive, but the more it costs. Hard disks are 10 to 30 times faster than CD-ROMs.

ACCESSORIES

Handy little tools which come with an operating system like Windows, that you can pop up on your screen whenever you need them. Examples include a calculator, notepad, and calendar.

ACTIVE CELL

The cell where you can enter numbers or formulas in a spreadsheet. The active cell has a thick border, and its name appears at the top of your screen, imaginatively called something like B3. Also known as the current cell.

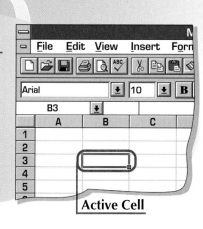

Active Cell

ACTIVE MATRIX SCREEN

A type of screen used in portable computers that displays bright, rich colors. It is easy to view from an angle, which makes it ideal for delivering presentations to several people. Also known as a Thin-Film Transistor (TFT) screen.

ACTIVE WINDOW

A window is a rectangular box on your screen. The active window is the one you are currently using, which appears on top of your other windows – making it the king of the hill.

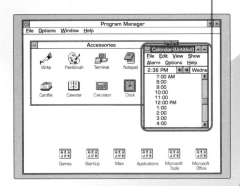

ADAPTER

See EXPANSION CARD.

AGENT

See INTELLIGENT AGENT.

AI (ARTIFICIAL INTELLIGENCE)

Computer software that can mimic the way human beings think. At one time, computer scientists thought this would be easy, but they haven't quite got the hang of it yet. Instead, most computers still exhibit a fair degree of artificial stupidity.

ALARM

A beep, bop, or balooa from your computer to let you know (a) you just did something it really didn't appreciate, or (b) your 3 o'clock should be waiting for you at reception.

ALGORITHM

A fancy name for a set of instructions like adding 2 and 2. Software uses algorithms, which spell out how to do the simplest things in painful detail, because computers are still a little, you know, dumb.

An Algorithm for Adding 2+2

```
10 START TASK
20 X=2
   Y=2
   X+Y=Z
50 PRINT Z
60 END TASK
```

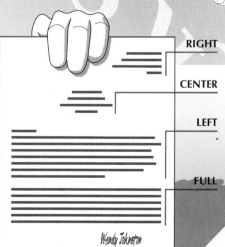

RIGHT

CENTER

LEFT

FULL

ALIGNMENT

How your text fits between the left and right margins of a page. Your text can be right-aligned, centered, left-aligned, or fully-aligned. Also called justification.

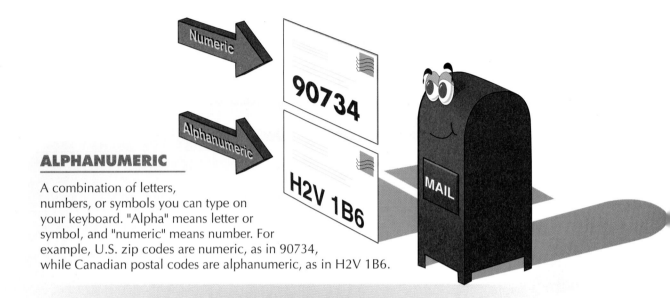

ALPHANUMERIC

A combination of letters, numbers, or symbols you can type on your keyboard. "Alpha" means letter or symbol, and "numeric" means number. For example, U.S. zip codes are numeric, as in 90734, while Canadian postal codes are alphanumeric, as in H2V 1B6.

ALT KEY

The key you can use to give an "alternate" set of commands. Alt commands are written Alt+X, which means hold down Alt while you press X. Alt commands are commonly used as shortcuts. For example, pressing Alt+F4 closes your active window faster than selecting Exit from the File menu.

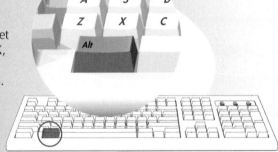

AMERICA ONLINE
INFORMATION SERVICE

A popular online service you can dial up with your modem, for a fee. People use America Online to exchange e-mail, look up information, chat in discussion groups, play games, and even surf the World Wide Web. Like all commercial services, America Online is easier to get started with and more organized than the Internet. See also WORLD WIDE WEB.

ANALOG INFORMATION

Information sent as a picture or sign that humans can easily understand — like your gas gauge pointing to empty when you're miles from the next gas station.

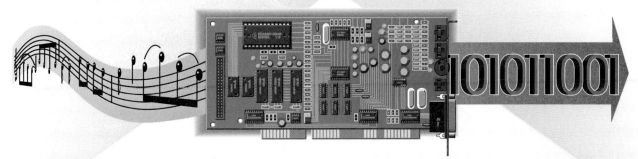

ANALOG-TO-DIGITAL (A/D) CONVERSION

Translating something that people can appreciate, like a piece of art or music, into a string of 1s and 0s that a computer can understand. For example, your sound card uses A/D conversion to turn music into computer files.

ANONYMOUS FTP

A way to transfer files between computers on the Internet without needing a password. Universities, government agencies, and companies around the world have made files available to the public. To transfer files using anonymous FTP, you sign in on the other computer as "guest" or "anonymous" instead of using your real name. See also FTP.

Anonymous FTP

Anti-Glare Screen – Archive

ANTI-GLARE SCREEN

A transparent screen that fits over the front of a monitor. It decreases the amount of light reflected off the computer screen to reduce eye strain.

ANTI-VIRUS SOFTWARE

Software viruses are annoying bits of code that can corrupt your program files. To protect your computer, you should use anti-virus software. This type of software is included with MS-DOS 6.2; or you can buy it separately at a computer store. See also VIRUS.

APM (ADVANCED POWER MANAGEMENT)

The smarts built into a portable computer to monitor and control its power consumption. APM puts your portable's screen or hard drive into "snooze" mode when you don't need them, so your batteries will last longer.

APPLICATION SOFTWARE

Programs that let you accomplish specific tasks. You can use application software to write letters, analyze numbers, sort files, manage finances, draw pictures, and even play games.

Some popular application software includes WordPerfect, Lotus 1-2-3, and Microsoft Access.

ARCHIE

As librarians of the Internet, Archie servers maintain catalogs of files found on various FTP sites on the Internet. To find the location of a file, just ask Archie and he'll point out which FTP site you can get it from. See also FTP.

ARCHIVE

To move seldom-used files from your hard drive to tape cartridges or floppy disks. Archiving old files frees up space on your hard drive. Then if you ever need a file you stored, you can retrieve it from the tape cartridge or floppy disk.

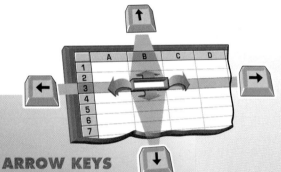

ARROW KEYS

The keys you use to move the cursor up, down, left, or right around your screen.

ASCII (AMERICAN STANDARD CODE FOR INFORMATION INTERCHANGE)

A universal code for text and numbers that all computers understand. ASCII makes it easy to exchange documents between different computers, or between different programs on the same computer. There's just one hitch: any formatting in your file — like tabs or bold letters — is lost when you save a file as ASCII.

ARTICLE

A piece of text contributed to a Usenet discussion group on the Internet. Usenet includes thousands of forums on every subject under the sun. Forum members can send in their articles by e-mail: anything from asking questions to including a topic for discussion. See also USENET.

REC. PETS

DOGS

Bear, my fourteen year old poodle is behaving oddly. Lately when I take him for a walk he will stop suddenly and roll on his back for several minutes. Should I be concerned?

Fish

Birds

Pigs

Cats

AUTO ANSWER

When your modem answers the phone by itself. You set the modem to auto answer when you know someone is just about to call you with their modem. The problem is, your mother usually calls first and gets the modem's piercing squeal in her ear.

AUTO-SAVE

When your computer thoughtfully saves your work every few minutes, all by itself. This gives you a backup copy in case you have any problems with your system, like a power failure. Check your manual to see if your program includes this feature.

AVI (AUDIO VIDEO INTERLEAVED)

A popular file format that combines video and audio. To play AVI files, you need Video for Windows. Windows' CD-ROMs contain AVI files that the computer uses to display video images.

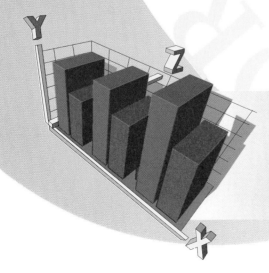

AXIS

One dimension of a chart, on which you can plot numbers. The horizontal line is called the X-axis, and the vertical line the Y-axis. Some spreadsheets also provide a third dimension of "depth" called the Z-axis.

Background Task – Bad Sector

BACKGROUND TASK

Most computers can do more than one thing at a time, like printing a report while you continue working on your screen. The computer handles the printing as a background task.

BACKLIT SCREEN

An internal light source at the back of a portable computer which makes the screen easier to view, especially in low-lit areas.

BACKSPACE KEY

The key on your keyboard labeled ←. You press the backspace key to back up and erase the character or space to the left of the cursor.

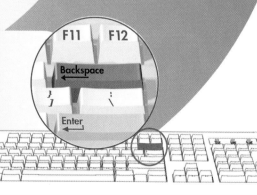

BACKUP

A copy made of a document onto a floppy disk or tape cartridge. This is done just in case the original gets lost, stolen, or deleted. Make backups regularly and according to what files you can't afford to lose. If you just finished or updated a 10 page report, due in a couple of days, make a backup — better to be safe than sorry.

BAD DISK

A floppy disk that no longer stores information reliably. If you have a bad disk, copy your work to another disk and throw out the floppy. Your information is worth more than the disk.

BAD SECTOR

A damaged portion of your floppy or hard disk that will no longer store information reliably. If your floppy disk has a bad sector, copy your work to another disk and discard the floppy. If your hard disk has a bad sector, you can run special software to isolate or "lock out" the sector.

Bandwidth –
Beta Test

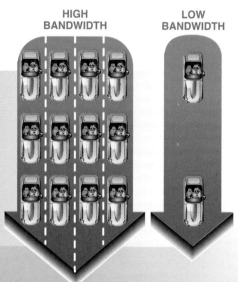

HIGH BANDWIDTH **LOW BANDWIDTH**

BANDWIDTH

How much information a network can carry. Think of the network as a highway, and each message as a car. The more lanes in the highway, and the higher the speed limit, the more traffic it can carry. So the wider the bandwidth of a network, and the faster its speed, the more information it can carry.

BATCH PROCESSING

A group of documents or files processed all at one time. For example, at the end of the day, you can collect all your reports and send them to the printer as one batch.

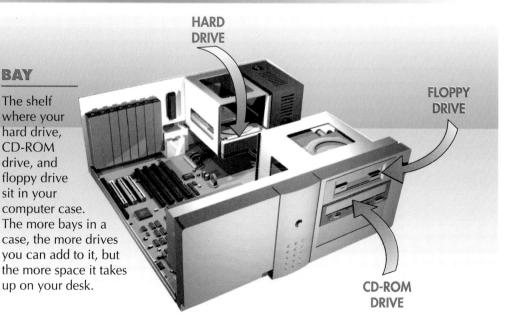

HARD DRIVE

FLOPPY DRIVE

CD-ROM DRIVE

BATTERY

See LITHIUM-ION, NICKEL CADMIUM, and NICKEL METAL HYDRIDE.

BAY

The shelf where your hard drive, CD-ROM drive, and floppy drive sit in your computer case. The more bays in a case, the more drives you can add to it, but the more space it takes up on your desk.

BBS (BULLETIN BOARD SYSTEM)

The electronic equivalent of a bulletin board where people can post notices for others with similar interests. People can dial up a BBS with their modems to exchange e-mail, computer files, and the latest gossip. Clubs and professional groups often sponsor their own BBS so members can exchange information and opinions.

BENCHMARK TEST

A standard test used to measure a computer's performance against its competitors. Many computer magazines put new machines through a set of benchmark tests to see which one earns their gold star.

BERNOULLI DRIVE

See REMOVABLE HARD DISK.

BETA TEST

An early version of a software product that's not quite ready for sale. Beta software is given to carefully selected users who try it out and report back any problems or suggested improvements.

BEZIER CURVE

An irregular curve you can create in a computer draw program. Bezier curves have handles you can move on the screen to adjust the curve's shape. Most of the drawings in this book were created using Bezier curves.

BINARY FILE

A file stored as a series of numbers and symbols that only computers can read. Games, applications, pictures, and music are all examples of binary files.

Will you marry me ?

BIOS (BASIC INPUT/OUTPUT SYSTEM)

A set of instructions stored in a ROM chip in your PC. The BIOS keeps track of all the peripherals and expansion cards in your system. After you switch on your computer, the BIOS runs an initial self-test and then starts the operating system. See also ROM.

BIT

A single number, either a 1 or 0, used for counting in the binary number system. A single bit can't tell you much, so bits are usually gathered into groups of 8 to make a byte. For instance, 8 bits can tell your computer you mean a certain letter, number, or symbol like M, 9, or $.

BITMAPPED FONT

A type style in which each character is stored as a pattern of dots. Changing the size of a bitmapped font results in visible distortions. Bitmapped fonts take up more storage space than outline fonts. See also OUTLINE FONT.

BITMAPPED IMAGE

A picture created by a pattern of tiny dots on the screen, called pixels. Bitmapped images require a lot of storage space and visibly distort if you change their size.

Block of Text – Boot Disk

BLOCK OF TEXT

In a word processor, a chunk of text you select so you can cut, copy, or move it all in one step. The block you select is highlighted to stand out on your screen.

BOARD

See EXPANSION CARD.

BOILERPLATE

Some all-purpose text you can type in once, save, and then recycle in many other documents. For example, a Casanova could reuse a boilerplate love letter every time he meets someone new.

BOLD

Characters shown with thicker, darker strokes. Putting a word in **bold** gives it **more oomph**.

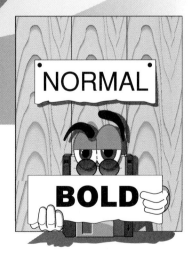

NORMAL

BOLD

B

BOOLEAN LOGIC

A powerful way to search for information using the words AND, OR and NOT. Boolean logic was created 150 years ago by English mathematician George Boole. Here's how you could use Boolean logic to find all the red or blue cubes in an assorted set of objects: find "Red" OR "Blue" AND "Cube".

BOOT OR BOOT UP

To start up a computer and load its operating system. Comes from the old saying "to pull yourself up by your bootstraps" which describes how a computer slowly wakes up after you turn it on.

BOOT DISK

A floppy disk with all the system software you need to start up your computer, in case you have a problem and can't boot up from your hard disk. Also called a bootable disk.

BPS (BITS PER SECOND)

The rate used to measure how fast a modem can send information over a telephone wire. Three popular modem speeds are 9,600 bps, 14,400 bps, and 28,800 bps. The higher the bps, the faster the modem. Faster modems may cost more, but they can also save you long distance charges by transmitting your files faster.

BRIDGE

A device that separates two networks to make traffic flow efficiently. A bridge allows a message across only if it's addressed to the other side, like from Sales to Accounting. Without a bridge, a message between two Sales people might be sent on a roundabout route all the way through Accounting and back.

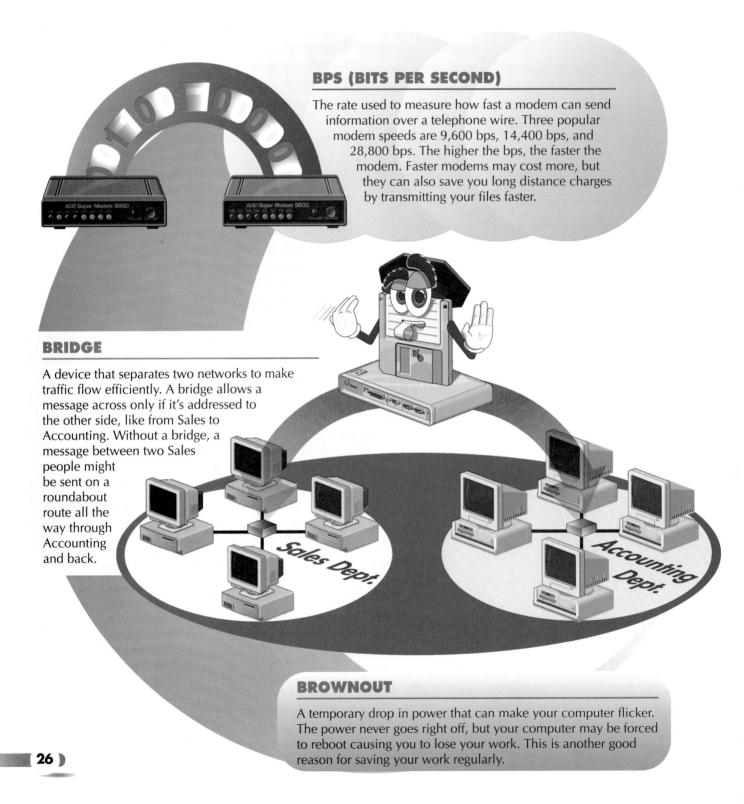

Sales Dept.

Accounting Dept.

BROWNOUT

A temporary drop in power that can make your computer flicker. The power never goes right off, but your computer may be forced to reboot causing you to lose your work. This is another good reason for saving your work regularly.

BROWSER

Software used to surf the World Wide Web. The Web has intriguing information on individuals, companies, and products from around the world. Using a browser, you can access text, graphics, sound, and even video. Two popular browsers are Mosaic and Netscape. See also MOSAIC, NETSCAPE, and WORLD WIDE WEB.

BUFFER

See PRINT BUFFER/ PRINT SPOOLER.

BUG

A mistake in the design of a computer's hardware or software. The first batch of Pentium CPU chips contained a bug that made them divide certain numbers incorrectly. With the incredible complexity of today's computers, it's almost impossible to develop a 100% bug-free product. Most serious bugs are quickly fixed by the manufacturer.

BULLETIN BOARD SYSTEM

See BBS.

Bundled Software – Byte

BUNDLED SOFTWARE

Software that comes free with a new computer. Computers for the home market usually come with all the basics you will need, such as word processing, database, spreadsheet, graphics, and electronic mail software. Some computers also come "bundled" with a CD-ROM encyclopedia or other multimedia software.

BURN-IN

When new computers are left running by a manufacturer for several days to find any problems before the machines are shipped.

BUS

An electronic pathway inside a computer, carrying information between the main CPU chip and expansion cards. Every PC contains several buses, which determine the types of expansion cards you can use with your computer. See also ISA BUS, PCI BUS, and VL-BUS.

BUSY FILE

A file in a computer that's already being used by someone else. If you try to open a busy file, the computer prevents you from doing so — just like getting a busy signal when you call someone who's already on the phone.

B

BUTTON

A little box on your screen that you click on to accomplish a task. Most buttons contain little pictures (icons) that display what they do, like a little printer you click on to print a document.

BUTTON BAR

A horizontal strip of buttons near the top of a window that provides shortcuts for commonly used commands. Some programs let you hide or display the button bar, and even mix and match buttons to create a personal button bar. Also called a toolbar.

BYTE

A set of 8 bits that means something to the computer, like a letter, number, or punctuation mark. For example, the byte 01001000 means a capital "H".
See also BIT and MEMORY CAPACITY.

C: Prompt – Caddy

C: PROMPT

See COMMAND PROMPT.

CACHE (DISK)

A section of RAM that allows your computer to operate faster.

Retrieving data from your hard disk is a slow process. A disk caching program helps solve this problem by placing recently used data in your disk cache.

Next time you need data, it may already be available in the disk cache, so a time-consuming search of the slow hard disk is avoided.

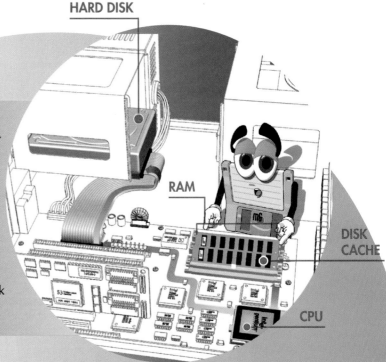

HARD DISK

RAM

DISK CACHE

CPU

CACHE (RAM)

RAM

Two groups of extremely fast memory chips that allow your computer to operate faster.

Internal cache (L1) is built into the CPU, and external cache (L2) resides on the motherboard. Both L1 and L2 store data recently used by the CPU. When the CPU needs data, it first checks the fastest source — L1. If the data is not there, the CPU checks the next-fastest source — L2. If the data still cannot be found, a time-consuming search of the slower RAM is required.

Note: L2 cache is also called SRAM.

CPU

L1 CACHE

L2 CACHE

CACHE HIT

When your computer successfully finds the data it needs in the cache. The greater the number of cache hits, the faster your computer operates. The opposite is a cache miss, when the data is not found in the cache. See also CACHE (DISK) and CACHE (RAM).

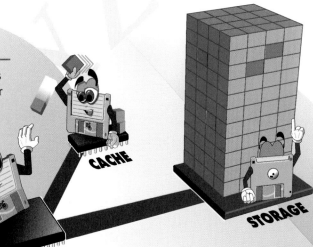

CACHE

CPU

STORAGE

CAD (COMPUTER-AIDED DESIGN)

A system that lets a designer use a computer screen instead of a drafting table to make plans and blueprints. Designers can use CAD for anything from the largest building to the tiniest screw. Not only is the CAD system capable of generating a 3-D illustration of a building, but it can also calculate how much building material is needed.

CADDY

The plastic and metal case where you put a CD-ROM before inserting it into a CD-ROM drive. Not all CD-ROM drives need caddies, but they do protect your CD-ROMs from dust and fingerprints — so they're great for households with lots of kids and pets.

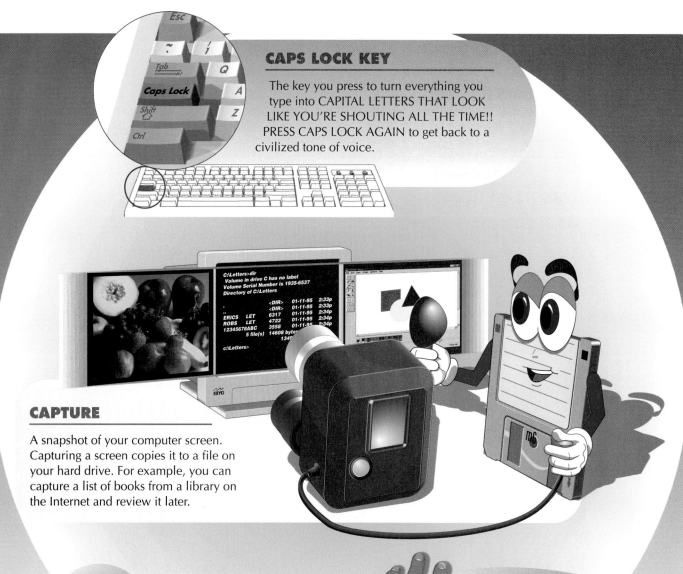

CAPS LOCK KEY

The key you press to turn everything you type into CAPITAL LETTERS THAT LOOK LIKE YOU'RE SHOUTING ALL THE TIME!! PRESS CAPS LOCK AGAIN to get back to a civilized tone of voice.

CAPTURE

A snapshot of your computer screen. Capturing a screen copies it to a file on your hard drive. For example, you can capture a list of books from a library on the Internet and review it later.

CARD

See EXPANSION CARD.

CARPAL TUNNEL SYNDROME

A condition of numbness, tingling, and pain in the fingers. It affects workers who type without proper wrist support or type for long periods of time without breaks.

CASCADE

A way to arrange all your open windows on your screen so that they overlap neatly, with just the title bars peeping out to show their names.

TOWER CASE

DESKTOP CASE

CASE

A box that contains all the major components of a computer system. A desktop case usually sits on a desk, under a monitor. A tower case usually sits on the floor.

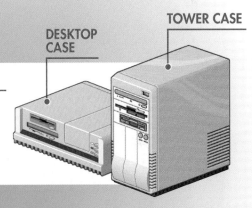

CASE SENSITIVE

A function found in most word processors or databases which can distinguish between upper and lower case letters. This is useful if you want to search for "PARROT" but skip over "parrot".

lowercase	UPPERCASE
i wish to complain about this parrot	I WISH TO COMPLAIN ABOUT THIS PARROT

CBT –
Character-Based Interface

CBT (COMPUTER-BASED TRAINING)

Using an interactive computer program to help teach new skills. Students like CBT because it lets everyone work at their own pace. CBT is also called "courseware."

CD-ROM (COMPACT DISC – READ ONLY MEMORY)

A silvery plastic disc that looks just like a music CD. Though it fits in the palm of your hand, a single CD-ROM can hold more information than a whole set of encyclopedias!

Because of their huge storage capacity, CD-ROMs are often used to distribute software and multimedia.

CELL

A box in a spreadsheet or table where you can enter information. Each cell in a spreadsheet has its own address, such as B3.

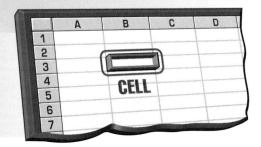

CELL ADDRESS

The location of a cell in a spreadsheet. A cell address consists of a column letter (A) followed by a row number (1). Together they make A1. Also called a cell reference.

CHARACTER

Any letter, number, or symbol you can type on your keyboard.

Character

Dear John:
I just bought a new computer. My letters to yo
late, but at least now
be printouts instead of me
handwriting!

Dave

Dear Mr. Muellejans:

We have developed a new training method for teaching word processing software. Our books integrate text and graphics to present concepts that are difficult to explain with text alone.

I look forward to showing you how the process works at our meeting this coming Friday.

Debbie Lang

Doc 1 Pg 1 Ln 1" Pos 1"

CHARACTER-BASED INTERFACE

Old-fashioned MS-DOS programs that display characters and even menus on the screen, but no graphics or buttons you can click on. Popular software like Lotus 1-2-3 Release 2.3 for DOS and WordPerfect 5.1 for DOS have character-based interfaces.

CHECK BOX

A little square in a dialog box you can click on to turn a certain feature on or off. When you see an X in the box, the feature is on. When the box is empty, the feature is off.

CHECKSUM

A simple mathematical test to verify that information was transmitted and received without error. Checksums are commonly used in modem software.

CHIP

A small piece of silicon containing millions of tiny electronic components. The tremendous miniaturization inside chips makes today's personal computers possible. Also called an integrated circuit (IC). Two common types of chips are CPU and RAM.

CIRCULAR REFERENCE

A common mistake in a spreadsheet, when a cell contains a reference to itself. For example, you might accidentally put the formula A1+A2+A3 into cell A3, in effect asking the spreadsheet to add A3 to A3. The spreadsheet goes around in circles for a while and finally admits it can't figure out what to do.

CLEAR

A function that erases information from a document. For example, if you want to delete some numbers in your spreadsheet, you can use "clear".

CLICK OR CLICK ON

Click means to press and release a button on your mouse. Click on means to move the mouse pointer over a certain object on your screen and then press and release the mouse button.

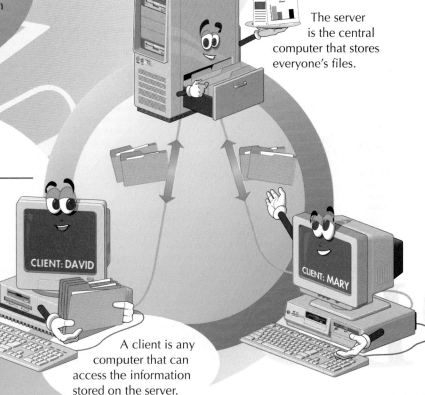

The server is the central computer that stores everyone's files.

CLIENT/SERVER NETWORK

The most efficient way to connect 10 or more computers in a network to share information.

Two popular client/server systems are Novell's NetWare and Microsoft's Windows NT.

A client is any computer that can access the information stored on the server.

Clip Art – Cluster

CLIP ART

Ready-made drawings you can add to your documents or presentations. Clip art can include items such as cartoons, maps, symbols, and flags. Clip art is included with some software packages or you can buy it separately.

CLIPBOARD

A temporary storage area in your computer that holds the last piece of information you cut or copied: text, numbers, or graphics. You can paste whatever is in the clipboard into your document.

CLOCK SPEED

The speed at which a computer runs, usually given in millions of cycles per second (Megahertz). Every system has a clock that drives its CPU at a fixed speed. Around 1980, computers ran at 4 Megahertz — now for the same money you can buy a 120 Megahertz computer. See also MEGAHERTZ.

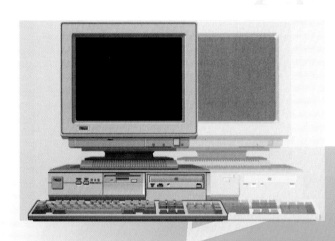

CLONE

An imitation of another computer that looks and works pretty much the same. Most PCs in existence are clones of models from name-brand manufacturers like IBM. People usually buy clones because they cost less than name-brand machines.

CLOSE

To shut down and remove a window or document from your screen.

CLUSTER

The smallest part of a disk, used by a PC to store information. No matter how tiny a file is, it still takes up at least one cluster on your disk.

COAXIAL CABLE

A high-quality cable used to connect computers in networks, similar to the wire between your VCR and TV.

CODEC (COMPRESSION/DECOMPRESSION)

A two-step process for compressing and decompressing huge files. First, a multimedia publisher uses a **co**dec to squeeze more sound and video into less space. These compressed files are easier to fit on a CD-ROM and transfer to your computer. Then, your computer uses a co**dec** to expand these files back to their original size and replay them on your screen. Two popular codecs are MPEG and Indeo.

COLLAPSE A VIEW

To condense a document or presentation so you see only your main headings and hide the remaining text. Also, to change the view of your files so you see only your main directories (folders) and nothing else.

- □ SELLING REAL ESTATE
  Mary Kurys
- □ OBJECTIVE
  - ● *State the desired objective*
  - ● *Use multiple points if necessary*
- □ CUSTOMER REQUIREMENTS
  - ● *State the needs of the audience*
  - ● *Confirm the audience's needs if you are not su...*
- □ MEETING THE NEEDS
  - ● *List the products and features, and how each addresses a specific need*
  - ● *This section may require multiple slides*
- □ COST ANALYSIS
  - ● *Point out financial benefits to the customer*
  - ● *Compare cost-benefits between you and your competitors*

- □ SELLING REAL ESTATE
- □ OBJECTIVE
- □ CUSTOMER REQUIREMENTS
- □ MEETING THE NEEDS
- □ COST ANALYSIS

COLOR DEPTH

The number of colors your PC can display on the screen. The more colors you have, the better everything looks on-screen, but the more the screen costs and the slower your computer runs. You need at least 256 colors for multimedia.

Bits	Colors
4	16
8	256
16	65,536
24	16.7 million

16 COLORS

16.7 MILLION COLORS

COLOR MAP OR COLOR PALETTE

A grid displaying all the colors available in a certain program. For example, in Excel 5 for Windows, you can choose from 56 colors to apply to your chart.

COLOR SEPARATION

The process of separating a picture by color to prepare it for professional printing. A full color document requires four separations: cyan, magenta, yellow, and black. Each separation indicates where the ink for that color will print to reproduce the original image.

CYAN

MAGENTA

YELLOW

BLACK

Column –
Computer-Aided Design

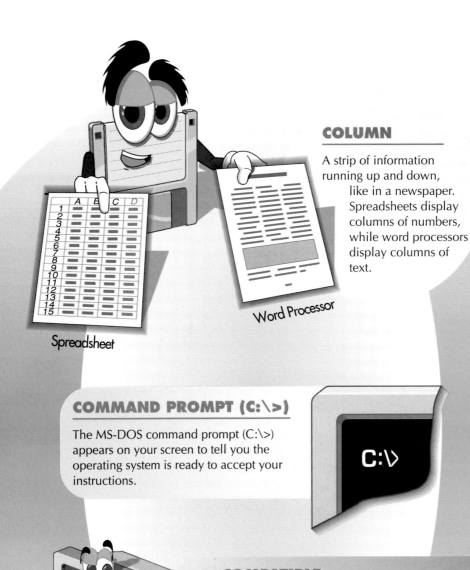

COLUMN

A strip of information running up and down, like in a newspaper. Spreadsheets display columns of numbers, while word processors display columns of text.

Word Processor

Spreadsheet

COMMAND PROMPT (C:\>)

The MS-DOS command prompt (C:\>) appears on your screen to tell you the operating system is ready to accept your instructions.

C:\>

COMPATIBLE

Pieces of software or hardware that get along well together. Compatible items share the same standards and speak the same language, so they can live together happily ever after.

COMPOUND DOCUMENT

A document that contains information from two or more programs. For example, a compound document can include text from a word processor, a graphic from a draw program, a chart from a spreadsheet, and a table from a database.

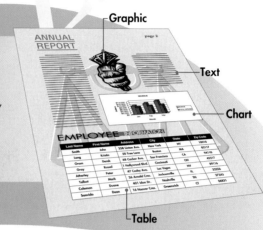

Graphic
Text
Chart
Table

COMPRESSION

Squeezing computer files into less space. Compressed files are handy because you can transmit them to another PC in less time, or store them on your hard disk in less space. When you need a compressed file, you can expand it back to its original size. Two popular compression programs are PKZIP and Stacker.

COMPUSERVE INFORMATION SERVICE

The largest online information service, with more than 3 million members worldwide. For a monthly fee, you can use a modem to call CompuServe and get news, send e-mail, do research, and access the Internet. For an hourly fee, you can access technical support on software, forums on careers and hobbies, and well-organized databases.

COMPUTER-AIDED DESIGN

See CAD.

CONFIGURATION

Hooking up different parts of a computer system so they all work together. Installing a sound card, CD-ROM drive, or fax modem in a PC used to take a lot of time and expertise. The Plug and Play feature of Windows 95 promises to reduce these hassles. See also PLUG AND PLAY.

CONNECT TIME

The amount of time your computer is connected to an online service, the Internet, or another computer. Commercial services like CompuServe often charge by the hour for connect time, and let you stay connected for as long as you want. Non-profit bulletin boards may limit you to an hour of connect time per day so that other people can get through.

CONTEXT-SENSITIVE HELP

A feature in a program that gives you help on the command or dialog box you're currently using. This saves you the time of searching through many screens and menus looking for answers.

C

CONTROL KEY (CTRL)

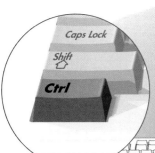

A key you can use to give you another set of commands. Ctrl commands are commonly used shortcuts. For example, pressing Ctrl+S in many programs saves your document faster than selecting Save from the File menu.

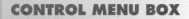

CONTROL MENU BOX

In Windows 3.1, the little box at the top left corner of every window. You can double-click on this box to close the window.

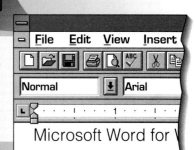

| File | Edit | View | Insert |

Normal — Arial

Microsoft Word for V

This screen displays wha
Microsoft Word for Windo

CONTROL PANEL

A window you can open to adjust various parts of your computer. You can use the Control Panel to adjust how fast your mouse moves, the colors on your screen, the volume of your speakers, the time and date on your computer, and so on.

COPY

To make an exact copy of information in your document so you can place the duplicate in a new location. Also, to make an exact copy of a file so you can place the duplicate on a different drive.

COPY PROTECTION

Any scheme developed by software manufacturers to stop people from making unauthorized copies of their software. Copy protection can be anything from a serial number you enter to access a program, to a special hardware "key" you insert into the back of your computer. See also PIRACY.

CORRUPTED FILE

A file so damaged that your computer can no longer read it. Many things can corrupt a file: your computer might crash or get infected with a virus. Once a file is corrupted, you can only restore it from a backup.

CPS (CHARACTERS PER SECOND)

A measurement of how fast a dot matrix printer prints. The higher the CPS, the faster the printer, but the more it costs.

CPU (CENTRAL PROCESSING UNIT)

The main chip in your computer. Even faster than the genius in your math class, the Central Processing Unit can do millions of calculations per second! Your programs use all this calculating power to help you do useful things like write letters and balance your checkbook.

CRASH

When your computer suddenly stops working. The screen usually freezes and you can't use your mouse or keyboard. When this happens, try restarting your computer by pressing Reset.

CRC (CYCLICAL REDUNDANCY CHECK)

A test used to verify that a message was received correctly. Telecommunications software uses a CRC to help detect and correct transmission errors.

CROSS-PLATFORM

A program available for more than one type of computer. For example, Microsoft produces the Word program for the PC platform and for the Macintosh platform. Using a cross-platform program makes it easier to exchange a document from one platform (computer) to another.

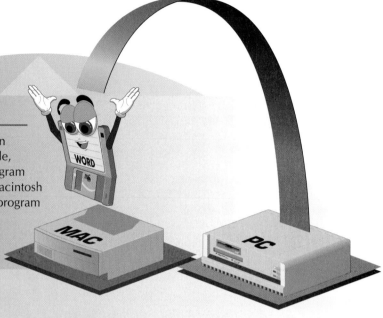

CTRL+ALT+DELETE

The three keys you press at the same time to reboot your PC, sometimes called a "warm boot." If your computer crashes, try doing this before you press the Reset button. See also CRASH.

CURRENT

The cell, directory, or drive where you are currently working. Also called active.

CURSOR

Where the action is on your screen, shown by a flashing line. When you type something on your keyboard, the information appears at the cursor.

Dear Mr. Johnston:

MICROSOFT WORD for Windows includes many new exciting features. A short demonstration of this software is schedule!

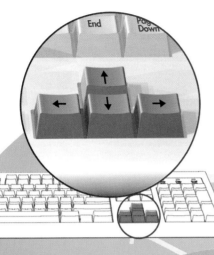

CURSOR KEY

A key marked with an arrow on your keyboard, used to move the cursor around your screen. A mouse can be faster, but the cursor keys are sometimes better for fine positioning.

CUT

To remove information but keep it around so you can paste it back in somewhere else: either in a new spot in the same document, or in a different document.

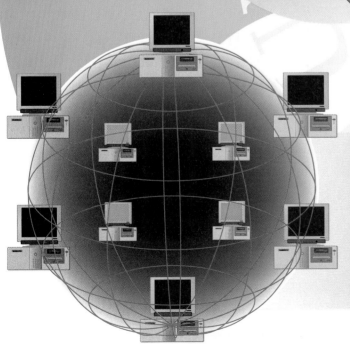

CYBERSPACE

A word coined by science-fiction author William Gibson to mean the electronic space created when many computers are connected together. In the future, cyberspace could become a multi-dimensional experience, where you hear sound and speech, and view and interact with 3-D objects.

DAT (DIGITAL AUDIO TAPE) DRIVE

A DAT drive is used to back up large amounts of information, such as all the files on a network. A DAT cartridge can store up to 8 Gigabytes of information (the equivalent of 10 or more CD-ROM discs). See also QIC DRIVE.

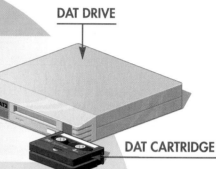

DAT DRIVE

DAT CARTRIDGE

DATA COMPRESSION

See COMPRESSION.

DATA SERIES

In a spreadsheet, a group of related information, such as the revenue for the last three months. You can create a chart from a data series to help spot trends.

DATA TRANSFER RATE (CD-ROM DRIVES)

The speed at which a CD-ROM drive can transfer information, usually given in Kilobytes per second (KB/s). The higher the data transfer rate, the faster the drive, but the more it costs. A faster CD-ROM drive can show smoother videos on your screen, and find information quicker on your CD-ROMs.

600 KB/s

CD-ROM Drive

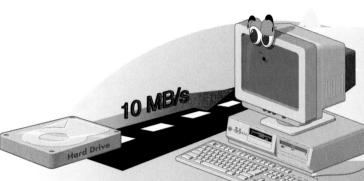

DATA TRANSFER RATE (HARD DRIVES)

The speed at which a hard drive can transfer information, usually given in Megabytes per second (MB/s). The higher the data transfer rate, the faster the drive, but the more it costs. A faster hard drive can save and open your files quicker, and help your system respond swiftly to your commands.

DATA TRANSFER RATE (MODEMS)

The speed at which a modem can transfer information, usually given in bits per second (bps). The higher the data transfer rate, the faster the modem, but the more it costs. A faster modem can save you money by cutting down on your long-distance charges. Three common speeds for modems are 9,600 bps, 14,400 bps, and 28,800 bps.

DATABASE

A program that helps you manage large collections of information. You can use a database to store, sort, and easily find information. Two popular database programs are Lotus Approach and Microsoft Access. See also FLAT FILE DATABASE and RELATIONAL DATABASE.

DB CONNECTOR

A type of connector on the end of a computer cable, shaped like a D so it only fits in one way. DB-9 connectors have 9 pins and are used to connect a mouse. DB-25 connectors have 25 pins and are used to connect a printer.

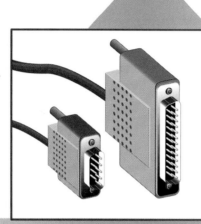

DBMS (DATABASE MANAGEMENT SYSTEM)

A fancy word for the expensive kind of software used by companies to keep track of all their records, often on a big computer called a mainframe. Two popular DBMS products are Oracle and Sybase. See also DATABASE.

DEBUG

To fix any serious mistakes (bugs) in a piece of software. Commercial software is usually debugged before it's shipped — just like vegetables.

DECRYPT

To decode a message that was coded for confidential purposes. To decode a message, you must have a special "key" such as a password. See also ENCRYPT.

DEFAULT

The initial setting on your computer. For example, the default font in Microsoft Word is 10 point Times New Roman — so everything you type appears in that font unless you instruct the computer otherwise.

DEFRAGMENT

A fragmented hard disk stores parts of a file in many different locations. To retrieve a file, the computer must search many areas on the disk. Defragmenting a disk places all the parts of a file in one location. This reduces the time the computer will spend locating the file. Windows 95 and MS-DOS 6.2 both include defragmenting software.

DELETE A FILE

To throw away a file you no longer need. If you're lucky, you can still recover a file that you deleted by mistake. See also RECOVER.

DELETE KEY

A key you can press to erase characters. On a PC, you press Delete to erase the character or space to the right of the cursor.

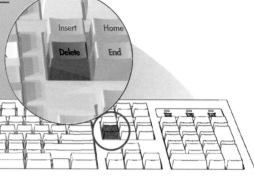

DEMO

A free sample of a program given out on a CD-ROM or floppy disk. The sample gives you just enough of a taste to entice you to buy the program. For example, game demos permit you to play only a few levels, to catch your interest.

DESELECT

To cancel the last item you selected. For example, you can deselect text in a word processor by clicking outside the selected area. See also SELECT TEXT.

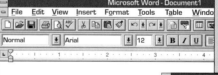

MICROSOFT WORD for Windows includes many new exciting features. A short demonstration of this software is scheduled for next Friday at 11:00 a.m. in the conference room.

MICROSOFT WORD for Windows includes many new exciting features. A short demonstration of this software is scheduled for next Friday at 11:00 a.m. in the conference room.

"click"

DESKTOP

On a PC, the background behind all your windows, menus, and dialog boxes, which is supposed to represent a desk. You can control whether your desktop is a neutral pattern, or a wild piece of art.

DESKTOP CASE

See CASE.

DESKTOP PUBLISHING

Using a computer to create impressive documents by combining text and graphics on the same page. You can use desktop publishing software to create newsletters, brochures, manuals, advertisements, books, and magazines. Two popular desktop publishing programs are Pagemaker and QuarkXPress.

DESTINATION

The drive, directory, or file towards which you are moving or copying a file. For example, if you want to copy a file from your hard drive to a floppy disk, the floppy disk is the destination.

Device Driver – Digital-To-Analog Conversion

DEVICE DRIVER

A special piece of software that translates between your operating system and a peripheral. For example, if you buy a new printer, you will need to install a new device driver to ensure the printer can communicate with your computer.

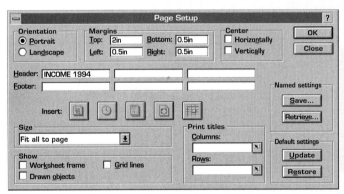

Page Setup					?

Orientation
- ● Portrait
- ○ Landscape

Margins
Top: 2in   Bottom: 0.5in
Left: 0.5in Right: 0.5in

Center
- ☐ Horizontally
- ☐ Vertically

OK
Close

Header: INCOME 1994
Footer:

Insert:

Named settings
Save...
Retrieve...

Size
Fit all to page

Print titles
Columns:
Rows:

Default settings
Update
Restore

Show
- ☐ Worksheet frame   ☐ Grid lines
- ☐ Drawn objects

DIALOG BOX

A box on your screen that lets you communicate with your computer. You can use a dialog box to enter information, set options, or give commands to your computer.

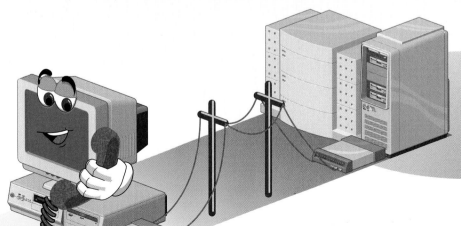

DIAL-UP

To access another computer by telephone, using your computer and modem.

DIGITAL CAMERA

Look Ma, no film! A digital camera takes pictures without film, and stores your snapshots as digital files in its memory. Later, you can transfer your picture files to your PC through a cable.

DIGITAL INFORMATION

Any information stored as a string of 1s and 0s that a computer can understand. For example, text, graphics, and sound are all stored as 1s and 0s in your computer.

DIGITAL-TO-ANALOG (D/A) CONVERSION

Translating a string of 1s and 0s from a computer (digital information) into analog information, such as sound, that a person can easily understand.

DIGITIZING TABLET

A pad that translates an artist's pen strokes into a computer graphic you can see on your screen. What it can't do is translate a quick doodle into a great piece of art.

Edit	
Undo Entry	Ctrl+Z
Can't Repeat	F4
Cut	Ctrl+X
Copy	Ctrl+C
Paste	Ctrl+V
Append	Ctrl+V
Select	

DIMMED

A menu option you can see but not choose, since it is not currently available. Dimmed options are shown in gray letters instead of black.

DINGBATS

Special characters like stars, hands, arrows, and geometric shapes you can use to decorate a document. A collection of dingbats is found in a popular font called Wingdings.

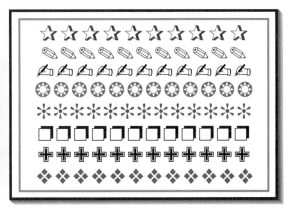

DIP (DUAL IN-LINE PACKAGE) SWITCHES

Tiny switches used to set how a piece of hardware works. You can adjust a DIP switch with the tip of a pen or a screwdriver — but you may want to get help from an experienced user. DIP switches are found on printers and modems.

DIRECTORY

Your computer stores programs and data in devices called drives. A drive contains directories to organize your information. Think of a drive as a filing cabinet and directories as drawers and folders. A directory usually contains related information. For example, the "Letters" directory contains all of your correspondence. Also called a folder.

DIRECTORY PATH

See PATH.

DIRECTORY TREE

See TREE.

DISK CACHE

See CACHE (DISK).

DISKETTE

See FLOPPY DISK.

DITHERING

Mixing dots of different colors on the screen to create the illusion of more colors than your monitor can normally display. This effect is available in some graphics programs.

DOCKING STATION

A piece of hardware that stays on your desk while you travel with a portable computer. When you return, you can pop your portable into a docking station to connect devices that your portable can't support, such as a larger screen, a CD-ROM drive, or a network. Docking stations are more expensive than port replicators. See also PORT REPLICATOR.

Program Manual

Documentation

DOCUMENTATION

Manuals, online help, README files, and any other instructions that come with a software package. Most people don't like flipping through manuals, but your documentation actually contains a surprising amount of information.

judy@sales.maran.com

INTERNET
12-27-95

DOMAIN

The part of an Internet address that identifies where a person's account is found. For instance, in the address **judy@sales.maran.com** the domain is everything after the @ — namely the **sales** computer in the **maran com**mercial organization. See also ZONE.

D

DOS

See
MS-DOS.

DOT MATRIX PRINTER

A noisy, yet relatively inexpensive type of printer. It uses a pattern of tiny dots to form images on a page, resulting in a low to moderate quality printout.

DOT PITCH

The size of the smallest dot (pixel) your screen can display. Dot pitch is usually given as a fraction of a millimeter, such as 0.28 mm or 0.35 mm. The smaller the dot pitch, the crisper the images are on the screen, but the more the screen costs.

0.28mm Dot Pitch

0.35mm Dot Pitch

Click
Click

DOUBLE-CLICK

To quickly press and release a button on your mouse twice.

Double-Density   High-Density

DOUBLE-DENSITY

720 PAGES

1,440 PAGES

Floppy disks come in two storage capacities: double-density and high-density. High-density disks store more information than double-density disks.

To tell them apart, a double-density floppy disk has only one hole at the top.

MicroFLOPPY Double Sided 720 K

MicroFLOPPY Double Sided 1.44 MB

Single - Spacing

Double - Spacing

DOUBLE-SPACING

To leave a blank line after every line of text. This is the preferred way to print manuscripts and school papers, but not business letters or documents — unless you are trying to stretch out a report.

DOUBLE-SPEED CD-ROM DRIVE

A CD-ROM drive that reads information twice as fast as a music CD. You need at least a double-speed (2X) drive to enjoy multimedia. Double-speed drives are slower but cost less than quad-speed drives.

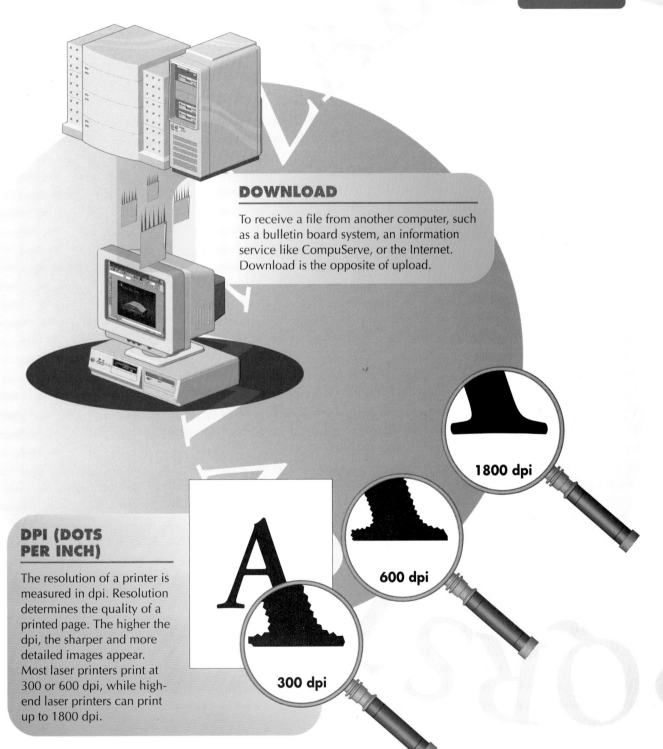

DOWNLOAD

To receive a file from another computer, such as a bulletin board system, an information service like CompuServe, or the Internet. Download is the opposite of upload.

DPI (DOTS PER INCH)

The resolution of a printer is measured in dpi. Resolution determines the quality of a printed page. The higher the dpi, the sharper and more detailed images appear. Most laser printers print at 300 or 600 dpi, while high-end laser printers can print up to 1800 dpi.

1800 dpi

600 dpi

300 dpi

Draft Mode – Draw Program

DRAFT MODE

A setting on a printer which produces a rough draft of a document. Printing in draft mode is faster, but doesn't look as sharp as other printing modes.

DRAG

To move an object around your screen. To drag an object, you point to it, press and hold down the mouse button, and then move the mouse.

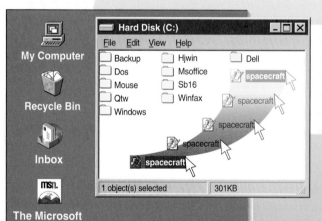

DRAG AND DROP

To move an object to a new spot on your screen, and then let it go. In Windows 95, you can delete a file by dragging and dropping it on the Recycle Bin.

DRAM

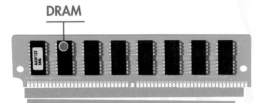

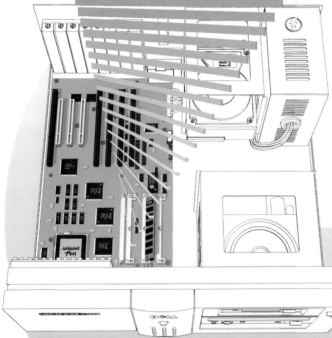

DRAM (DYNAMIC RANDOM ACCESS MEMORY)

The most common type of memory chip, used for the computer's main memory. All information stored in DRAM is temporary and is lost if there is a power failure. Adding DRAM is the most cost-effective way to improve the performance of a computer. Also called RAM.

DRAW PROGRAM

Software used to create any type of drawing, from a simple line sketch to a magnificent full-color poster. Draw programs are used by graphic artists and designers. For example, all the illustrations in this book were created with Adobe Illustrator, a popular draw program. See also PAINT PROGRAM.

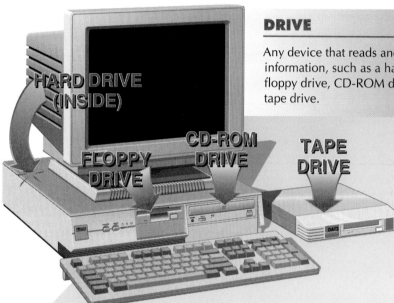

DRIVE

Any device that reads and writes information, such as a hard drive, floppy drive, CD-ROM drive, or tape drive.

HARD DRIVE (INSIDE)

FLOPPY DRIVE

CD-ROM DRIVE

TAPE DRIVE

DRIVE BAY

See BAY.

DRIVER

See DEVICE DRIVER.

DSP (DIGITAL SIGNAL PROCESSING) CHIP

A special type of chip that takes over some of the workload from a computer's main chip, the CPU. While the CPU does all the basic processing, the DSP handles the other jobs, such as compressing and expanding speech, music, and video files. As CPUs get more powerful in the future, DSP chips may no longer be needed.

DUAL-SCAN

The most inexpensive color screen for a portable computer. Dual-scan screens aren't as bright and don't work as well for multimedia as active matrix color screens, but they cost less and use less power. A dual-scan screen is also hard to view from an angle, which makes it ideal when you want to keep work private from people sitting next to you. See also ACTIVE MATRIX SCREEN.

DUMB TERMINAL

A screen and keyboard with no smarts of its own, like a bank's automated teller machine. Dumb terminals are completely dependent on the main computer they are connected to and are typically used for simple data entry and retrieval tasks.

DUPLEX

A circuit or telephone line that can do two things at once. With a full-duplex connection between modems, both modems can send and receive information at the same time. With a half-duplex connection, one modem has to receive before the other sends. Most communications software gives you a choice of either setting.

DVORAK KEYBOARD

A keyboard designed to make typing more efficient. The standard QWERTY keyboard was designed to slow down typists who kept jamming the early mechanical typewriters. This can't happen with a computer keyboard, but we'd all have to start from scratch to learn the Dvorak keyboard, so everyone goes on using the less-efficient QWERTY keyboards. See also QWERTY KEYBOARD.

DX/DX2/ DX4 CHIP

See
486DX,
486DX2, and
486DX4.

EIDE

See
ENHANCED IDE.

EJECT BUTTON

The button you press
to pop a floppy disk or
CD-ROM disc out of a
drive. Also, what James
Bond uses to get rid of
back-seat drivers.

E-MAIL
(ELECTRONIC MAIL)

Sending and receiving messages through
a computer network. To use electronic
mail, you need a computer, modem or
network connection, and an e-mail
address. E-mail is convenient because
all messages are sent and received
immediately, even over long
distances.

EMBEDDED
OBJECT

See OBJECT
LINKING AND
EMBEDDING.

EMOTICON

See SMILEY.

EMULATOR

Something that pretends to be something
else, usually a more popular type of
machine. For example, many printers
emulate more popular models, such as
the HP LaserJet. This lets your
computer communicate with the
printer as if it were a LaserJet.

ENCRYPT

To scramble a message or file for confidential purposes, so only the person who has the password can read the information. See also DECRYPT.

END KEY

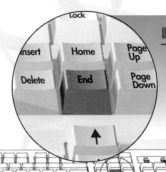

The key you press to move the cursor to the end of the current line. Many programs also use keyboard shortcuts such as Ctrl+End to move the cursor to the end of a document.

ENHANCED IDE (EIDE)

A way of connecting devices to a computer. EIDE can connect up to four devices, such as hard drives, CD-ROM drives, and tape drives. EIDE was developed to surpass its older brother IDE, which is slower and can only connect two hard drives. Most new computers come with EIDE. See also IDE.

ENTER KEY

The key you press to begin a new line in a word processor, or to enter information into a spreadsheet. Pressing "Enter" is the same as clicking OK in a dialog box. Also called Return Key.

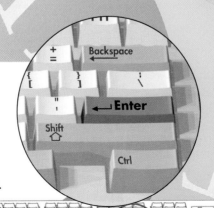

ERGONOMICS

The science of designing equipment for a comfortable and safe working environment. For example, an ergonomic chair is fully adjustable and provides support for your lower back.

ERROR CORRECTION

A method for finding and fixing errors in a transmission between computers. Error correction is built into communications software. Two popular standards for error correction are MNP 4 and V4.2.

ERROR MESSAGE

A message that appears on your screen to let you know that your computer cannot carry out your instructions.

E

ETHERNET

The most popular way to exchange information between computers on a network. Ethernet allows individuals to share files as well as peripherals such as a printer.

Ethernet works the same way people talk during a polite conversation. Each computer waits for a pause before sending information through the network. If two computers try to send information at the same time, a collision occurs. After a pause, the computers try to resend the information.

EUDORA

The most popular software you can use to sort your e-mail messages. Eudora classifies your messages as IN or OUT and lets you create additional mailboxes. For example, you can have Eudora sort your e-mail into groups called IN, OUT, PERSONAL, and BUSINESS. This saves you time because it allows you to quickly find certain messages, instead of searching through all your e-mail.

EXIT

To shut down a program or application when you have completed your work. In Windows, you can select the Exit command from the File menu.

EXPAND A VIEW

To change the view of your files so you see your main directories (folders) as well as any files inside them. Also, to change the view of a document or presentation so you see both your main headings and underlying text.

EXPANSION CARD

A circuit board you can install in your computer to add a new feature. For example, an expansion card can add CD-quality sound or a modem. Also called an expansion board.

EXPANSION SLOT

A socket on the motherboard where you can plug in an expansion card. The more expansion slots your computer has, the more features you can add. When you buy a computer, make sure the motherboard has enough expansion slots for your future needs. Also called an expansion bus.

EXPERT SYSTEM

A computer system that is programmed to mimic the procedures and decisions that "experts" make. For example, an expert system uses your monthly expenses, liabilities, income, assets, and credit history to determine if you meet the requirements for a loan.

EXTENSION

The last characters in a file name, after the period. The extension usually identifies the program used to create the file. For example, the PPT extension in SKYSCRAP.PPT identifies a PowerPoint document.

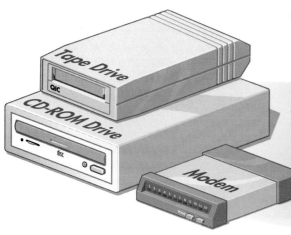

EXTERNAL

A device in its own box outside your computer case, such as an external modem, tape drive, or CD-ROM drive. External units cost more than internal ones, but they are more versatile, since you can easily move them to another computer.

FANFOLD PAPER

Continuous paper with holes on the edges, used by dot matrix printers. After you print on fanfold paper, you have to separate the pages and tear off the edge strips.

FAQ (FREQUENTLY ASKED QUESTIONS)

A file that contains a list of all the questions and answers that regularly appear on a newsgroup. The FAQ gives you an idea of the type of topics discussed in a newsgroup. It also prevents new readers from asking the same questions over and over again. Make sure you read the FAQ before posting any articles to a newsgroup.

FAX MODEM

A combination fax machine and modem you can use with your computer. A fax modem saves you time and paper, since you can fax a document straight from your computer, instead of printing it out and then faxing it. The downside is that you can't fax any notes or documents that aren't already in your computer.

FEMALE CONNECTOR

A computer plug that has holes. An example is a mouse plug that you insert into your computer.

FIBER OPTICS

Cables that contain thin strands of glass that carry light instead of electricity. Fiber optics are lighter, immune to electrical interference, and carry information faster than standard network cables. Fiber optics are used in high-speed computer networks.

FIELDS

Record 1
FIELD(Name): **Mr. John Smith**
FIELD(Address): **11 Linton Street**
FIELD(City, State): **Atlanta, GA**
FIELD(Zip Code): **30367**
FIELD(Salutation): **Mr. Smith**

FIELD

Separate but related pieces of information you can enter in a database, such as a name, address, city, state, zip code, or salutation. A complete set of fields is called a record.

FILE

A collection of information stored on your computer with its own name. You can use files to store text, numbers, graphics, sound, or video.

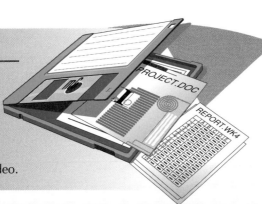

FILE FORMAT

The blueprint for building a certain type of file. Software programs like Microsoft Word and Lotus 1-2-3 each have a special file format they use to store information.

FILE NAME

A name you give to a file on your computer. MS-DOS and Windows 3.1 file names can be up to 8 characters long with a 3 character extension after the period (example: MYLETTER.DOC). These file names cannot include spaces. Windows 95 can use up to 255 characters to name a file, including spaces (example: GARDENING TIPS).

FILE SERVER

One central computer that stores the files for everyone connected to a network. Since all the files are stored together on the file server, they are easier to manage and protect.

FILTER

A feature in a spreadsheet program that allows you to narrow a list and display only the records containing the data you specify. For example, you can filter a list to display only the employees who sold more than 1,000 units last month.

FIND

See SEARCH.

FIREWALL

Special software designed to protect a private computer system from unauthorized access. Firewalls are used by corporations, banks, and research facilities on the Internet to keep hackers out. See also HACKER.

FLAME

To send angry or spiteful words over the Internet. Some people vent harsh opinions online, perhaps because they don't have to deal face-to-face with the other person.

Flash Memory – Folder

FLASH MEMORY

A type of memory that retains information even after you turn the power off. Flash memory is commonly used to store programs on portable computers.

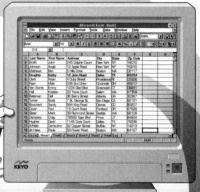

FLAT FILE DATABASE

A program you can use to manage a simple collection of information, such as an address book or list of phone numbers. With a flat file database, you can store, sort, and find your information quickly. Flat file databases are easy to set up and learn. See also DATABASE and RELATIONAL DATABASE.

FLATBED SCANNER

A device you can use to copy an image from paper onto your computer. Flatbed scanners work like photocopiers, but they create a computer copy instead of a paper copy. A flatbed scanner can import an entire page at once and produce clearer images than a hand-held scanner. See also HAND-HELD SCANNER.

FLOATING POINT UNIT (FPU)

See MATH COPROCESSOR.

FLOPPY DISK

A removable disk that stores information magnetically. You can use a floppy disk to exchange information between computers, or to make a backup of your files. Also called a diskette.

MicroFLOPPY
Double Sided
1.44 MB

Floppy disks come in two sizes: double-density and high-density. To protect your floppy disks, keep them away from heat, drinks, and magnets.
See also BACKUP, DOUBLE-DENSITY, and HIGH-DENSITY.

FM SYNTHESIS

The way that inexpensive sound cards produce sound. FM synthesis creates unrealistic, tinny sounds by imitating musical instruments. Sound cards that use FM synthesis cost less, but don't sound as rich as cards using wavetable synthesis. See also WAVETABLE SYNTHESIS.

FOLDER

An area of a disk that holds a group of documents. Like a folder in a filing cabinet, a folder lets you easily find and work with related documents. Also called a directory.

Font – Format a Disk

FONT

A set of characters with a particular design and size. You can choose from many different fonts to change the look of your work.

FONT CARTRIDGE

A small attachment you plug into a printer so you can use additional fonts in your printouts.

10 point
12 point
14 point
18 point
24 point
36 point

FONT SIZE

The size of the characters on your screen and printouts. There are 72 points to an inch. Regular type in newspapers, reports, and letters is usually 12 points or less.

FOOTER

Information displayed at the bottom of a page in a document. A footer can contain a page number, the date, your company name, or anything else you want to include.

PAGE 1

FOOTNOTE

A note at the bottom of a page to provide additional information about an item in a document. Footnotes often appear in scholarly journals and textbooks.

1. H. Smith, <u>Aeronautical Refrigeration Repair</u> (California: Quest Publishing, 1989) 10.

2. R. Anderson, <u>Volatile Cold Gases</u> (Alaska: Inert Publishing, 1992) 31.

FOOTPRINT

The amount of space a machine takes up on your desk, usually given in square inches. The smaller the footprint, the less desk space the machine occupies.

FORMAT A DISK

To prepare a floppy disk so that your computer can read and write information on it. Most floppy disks you buy today are already formatted for you. Sometimes called "initializing" a floppy.

Format a Document – Freenet

FORMAT A DOCUMENT

To improve the appearance of a document. Examples of formatting include changing the font, alignment, margins, line spacing, borders, and shading in a document.

Helvetica 24pt

FPU (FLOATING POINT UNIT)

See MATH COPROCESSOR.

FRACTAL

A mathematical formula used in computer graphics programs to draw objects with naturally recurring patterns, such as clouds, leaves, waves, or abstract images.

FRAGMENTATION

When you save a file to your hard disk, it tries to keep all clusters (parts of a file) together. This allows your computer to retrieve a file quickly. Eventually files are deleted from your hard disk. This leaves empty spaces between the remaining files.

If a large file is then saved, the hard disk must break the file apart and store clusters in empty spaces all over the disk. This process is called disk fragmentation. It then takes longer to access files from the hard disk. See also DEFRAGMENT.

CLUSTER

F

FREE SPACE

Empty space on a hard drive. If a program needs 10 Megabytes of free space, that means installing it will fill up 10 Megabytes of space on your hard drive.

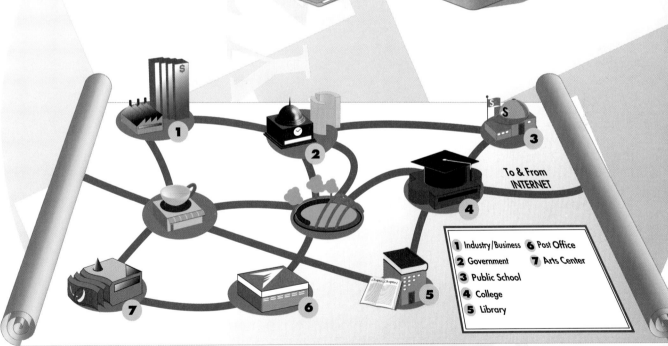

To & From INTERNET

1 Industry/Business 6 Post Office
2 Government 7 Arts Center
3 Public School
4 College
5 Library

FREENET

A public network that gives you free access to community news and information, as well as basic entry to the Internet. Think of a freenet as an electronic town since it has a post office for your e-mail, a library for research, and bulletin boards for community events. In 1986, Cleveland set up the first freenet. See also INTERNET.

FREEWARE

Software written by some generous-hearted programmer and then donated to the public, so anyone is free to copy it and give it to their friends. This is not the same as shareware or commercial software, which you are supposed to pay for.

FREQUENCY

How often something happens — most often used to describe how often a sound wave goes through its whole cycle from peak to trough. The more cycles, the higher the frequency, so the higher-pitched the sound. Frequencies are measured in cycles per second, or Hertz. Radio and TV frequencies are also measured in Hertz. See also HERTZ.

HIGH

LOW

FTP (FILE TRANSFER PROTOCOL)

A popular way to transfer files between computers on the Internet. Universities, government agencies, and companies around the world have FTP sites offering files that you can look through and copy to your computer using the file transfer protocol. See also ANONYMOUS FTP.

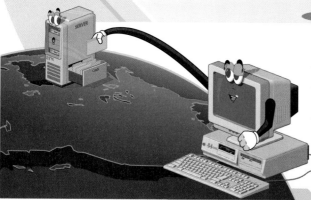

FULL DUPLEX

See DUPLEX.

FULL-MOTION, FULL-SCREEN VIDEO

WITHOUT MPEG

Most multimedia products play videos in tiny windows (not full-screen) with jerky movement (not full-motion) mainly because video files are so huge. No CD-ROM can transfer files to your computer fast enough to show video in full motion over your full screen. Instead, your computer shrinks the size of the video window and displays fewer frames per second. Displaying fewer frames causes the movement of images to appear jerky.

WITH MPEG

The only practical way to show full-motion, full-screen video is with a standard like MPEG. MPEG squeezes video into files that are easier to handle. This allows a CD-ROM to transfer these smaller files to your computer faster. Your computer then uses MPEG to decompress the files. This provides full-motion, full-screen video.

FUNCTION KEY

A key labeled from F1 to F12 that you can press to do a certain task. For example, in many programs, you can press F1 to display help information.

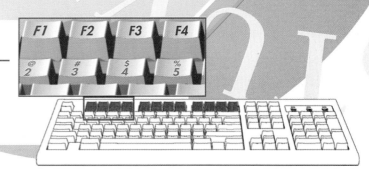

GAME PORT

A socket at the back of a computer where you can plug in a joystick. You can use a joystick with games to fly, drive, or shoot objects. See also JOYSTICK and PORT.

GHOSTING

A shadow of an image that lingers when you move the image on your screen. This occurs on inexpensive portable computer screens.

GIF (GRAPHICS INTERCHANGE FORMAT)

Pronounced "jiff." A file format for pictures, photographs, and drawings. GIF files are compressed so that you can send them across telephone lines quickly. GIF is widely used on electronic bulletin boards and the Internet. GIF files are limited to 256 colors, so they cannot be used for high-end desktop publishing.

GIGABYTE (GB)

See MEMORY CAPACITY.

G

GOPHER

A program that uses a menu system to help you find and retrieve information on the Internet. A Gopher menu displays a list of items. When you select an item, a new menu appears. Eventually, you will see the file you want to retrieve. See also VERONICA.

GRAMMAR CHECKER

A program often included in word processors that improves the accuracy of a document. It checks your punctuation, grammar, and writing style and recommends a better way to phrase any incorrect sentences.

GRAPH

A picture created from a set of numbers. Graphs can help you recognize trends that are not obvious in a simple list of numbers. Popular graph types include line, bar, area, and pie graphs. Also called a chart.

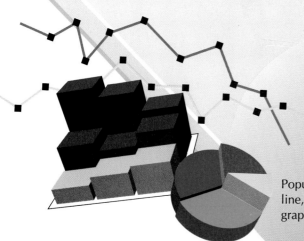

Green PC – GUI

GREEN PC

An energy-saving computer, printer, or monitor that enters a sleep mode when not used for a certain period of time. When you use the device again, it returns to full-power mode.

GRID LINES

The lines that separate cells in a spreadsheet.

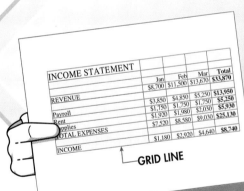

INCOME STATEMENT	Jan	Feb	Mar	Total
	$8,700	$11,500	$13,670	$33,870
REVENUE				
	$3,850	$4,850	$5,250	$13,950
Payroll	$1,750	$1,750	$1,750	$5,250
Rent	$1,920	$1,980	$2,030	$5,930
Supplies	$7,520	$8,580	$9,030	$25,130
TOTAL EXPENSES				
INCOME	$1,180	$2,920	$4,640	$8,740

← GRID LINE

GROUP ICON

In Windows, a picture on your screen that represents a window containing related items. You can click on a group icon to see its contents.

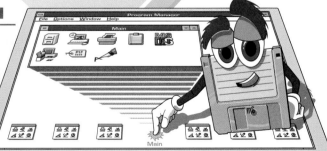

G

GROUPWARE

A type of software that helps improve the productivity of people working on a related project. Groupware lets several people work with the same file at once. It also helps coordinate and manage activities, such as scheduling meetings.

Windows 3.1

Windows 95

GUI (GRAPHICAL USER INTERFACE)

Pronounced "gooey." A type of display where you can see and point to what you want — like a kid in a candy store. Using the menus, windows, and icons in a GUI is much easier than typing complicated commands. Windows is a popular GUI.

89

HACKER

An ace programmer who can do almost anything with a computer. A few hackers test their skills by breaking into other people's computers with their modems. Some hackers cause havoc, while others just want to prove they can get past the security system.

HALF-DUPLEX

See DUPLEX.

HAND-HELD SCANNER

A portable device you can use to copy an image from paper to your computer. Hand-held scanners are ideal for capturing small images, such as signatures and logos. A hand-held scanner is smaller, less expensive, and more portable than a flatbed scanner. See also FLATBED SCANNER.

HANDLES

Little squares at the edges and corners of a selected graphic on your screen. You can move a handle with your mouse pointer to resize or reshape the graphic.

HANDLE

HANDSHAKE

Two modems perform a handshake each time
they meet, just as two people shake hands to
greet each other. If the modem speaker is on, you
can actually hear the handshake — it's that
annoying series of squeals and signals. The
handshake helps the modems determine
how they will exchange information.

HARD COPY

A printed copy of
the file displayed
on your screen.

Document

HARD DISK OR HARD DRIVE

The primary device that
a computer uses to store
information. Most computers
come with one hard drive,
called drive C, located
inside the computer case.
See also REMOVABLE
HARD DISK.

HARDWARE

Any part of a computer system that you can see or touch, such as a keyboard, screen, mouse, joystick, printer, speakers, and so on.

HEADER

Information displayed at the top of a page in a document. A header can contain a page number, the name of your company, the title of the report, or anything else you want to include.

HERTZ

A measurement of how fast your computer processes information. As software becomes more complex, increased computer speeds (or Hertz) become necessary. Modern Pentium (586) computers operate at 90 Megahertz (90,000,000 Hertz), while the ancient 286 computers operated at 12 Megahertz (12,000,000 Hertz).

1 HERTZ

30 HERTZ

One Second

One Second

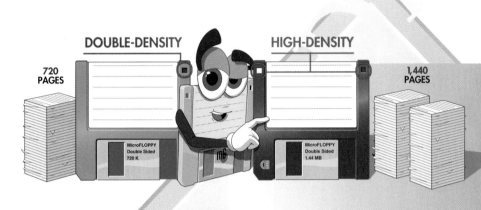

DOUBLE-DENSITY

720 PAGES

MicroFLOPPY Double Sided 720 K

HIGH-DENSITY

1,440 PAGES

MicroFLOPPY Double Sided 1.44 MB

HIGH-DENSITY

Floppy disks come in two storage capacities: high-density and double-density. High-density disks store more information than double-density disks.

To tell them apart, a high-density floppy disk has two holes at the top.

HIGHLIGHT

To select text or a graphic you want to alter. For example, you can bold, underline, delete, copy, or even move text that is highlighted.

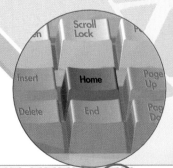

HOME KEY

The key you press to move the cursor to the beginning of the current line. Many programs also use keyboard shortcuts such as Ctrl+Home to move the cursor to the beginning of your document.

The White House

HOME PAGE

An introductory screen on the World Wide Web, used to welcome visitors. A home page can include special underlined text or graphics you click on to jump to related information on other pages on the Web. Many individuals, businesses, and organizations now have home pages on the World Wide Web. See also WORLD WIDE WEB.

HOST

The name given to any computer directly connected to the Internet. Host computers are usually associated with running computer networks, online services, or bulletin board systems (BBSs). In reality, a host computer on the Internet could be anything from a mainframe to a personal computer. See also BBS.

HTML (HYPERTEXT MARKUP LANGUAGE)

Software language used to create pages for the Internet's World Wide Web. It uses special links to connect related information (text, graphics, photographs, sound, and video) together. The links can connect to other items in the document or a Web site across the world. See also WORLD WIDE WEB.

HYPERMEDIA

A user-friendly way to connect related information (text, graphics, photographs, sound, and video). Hypermedia uses special "links" you can click on to jump from one related topic to another. For example, if you are viewing the home page of the White House, you can click on "The First Family" to jump to a photo of Bill and Hillary Clinton.

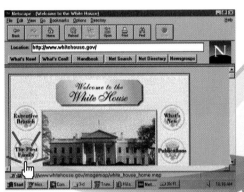

HYPERTEXT

A user-friendly way to connect related textual information. Hypertext uses special "links" you can click on to jump from one related topic to another. For example, when you click on "Quit Windows" in the Windows 3.1 help menu, you jump directly to a description of how to perform the task.

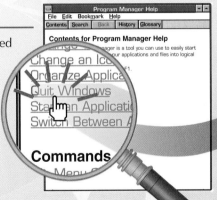

HYPHENATION

Breaking a word with a hyphen when the word touches the right margin on a page. Most word processors and desktop publishing programs automatically hyphenate, but you may not appreciate where they place the hyphens.

Breaking a word with a hyphen when it touches the right margin on a page. Most word pro-cessors and desktop publishing programs auto-matically hyphenate, but you may not appre-they place the hyphens.

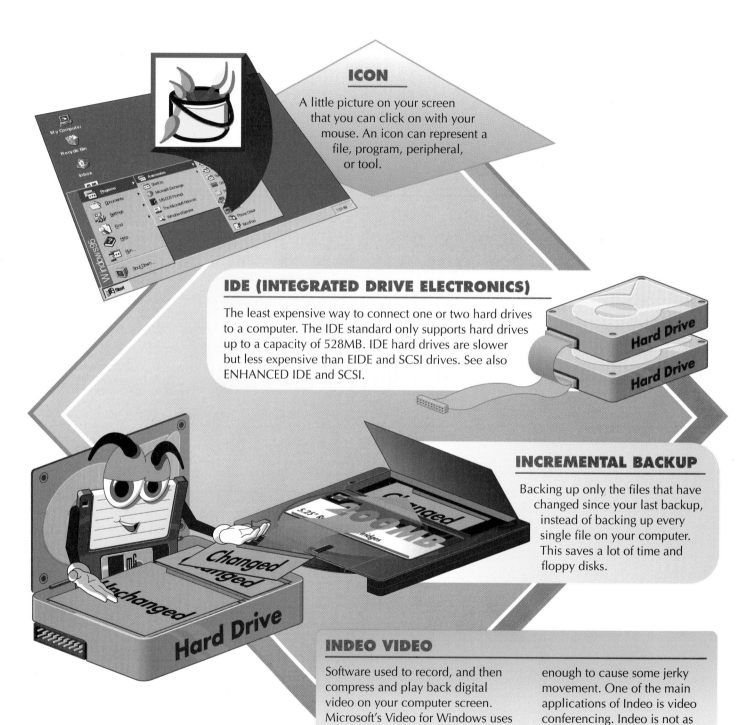

ICON

A little picture on your screen that you can click on with your mouse. An icon can represent a file, program, peripheral, or tool.

IDE (INTEGRATED DRIVE ELECTRONICS)

The least expensive way to connect one or two hard drives to a computer. The IDE standard only supports hard drives up to a capacity of 528MB. IDE hard drives are slower but less expensive than EIDE and SCSI drives. See also ENHANCED IDE and SCSI.

INCREMENTAL BACKUP

Backing up only the files that have changed since your last backup, instead of backing up every single file on your computer. This saves a lot of time and floppy disks.

INDEO VIDEO

Software used to record, and then compress and play back digital video on your computer screen. Microsoft's Video for Windows uses Indeo. Indeo plays back video over 1/4 of your screen (320x240 pixels) at 15 frames per second — slow enough to cause some jerky movement. One of the main applications of Indeo is video conferencing. Indeo is not as powerful as MPEG, but requires no extra hardware. See also CODEC.

INFORMATION SERVICE

See ONLINE SERVICE.

INFORMATION SUPERHIGHWAY

The vision of a global, high-speed network that people can use to exchange e-mail, study, get the news, and access vast amounts of business, government, and educational information. The information superhighway will also enable us to bank, shop, and plan vacations from our computers at home.

The Internet is the prototype of the information highway because it already provides many of these features. The rest are quickly becoming a reality, thanks to the growth of telephone networks, cable TV, service providers, and satellites.

INK JET PRINTER

A printer that produces high-quality documents for a relatively low cost. Ink jet printers work by squirting tiny drops of ink onto paper. Color ink jet printers are the least expensive type of color printer available. They are ideal for adding touches of color to a page, but not for reproducing color photos.

INPUT DEVICE

A device you can use to enter commands or information into your computer, such as a keyboard, mouse, joystick, modem, scanner, or microphone.

INSERT KEY

The key you can use, in most word processors, to switch between the insert and typeover modes. In the insert mode, the text you type pushes existing text forward to make room for the new text. In the typeover mode, the text you type replaces (types over) any existing text.

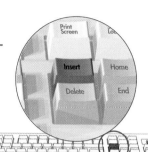

INTEGRATED SOFTWARE

Software that contains several applications rolled into one. Integrated software usually includes word processing, spreadsheet, database, graphics and communication capabilities. Two popular integrated software packages are Microsoft Works and ClarisWorks: both give you the "works" for a reasonable price.

INTELLIGENT AGENT

Software designed to work for you based on rules that define your preferences and requirements. For example, on its own, an intelligent agent can scan through databases and identify articles of interest to you, or compile all your weekly and monthly reports.

INTERACTIVE

A system that interacts with you as though you're having a conversation: you ask the system to do something and it responds. Most programs are somewhat interactive, with computer games and multimedia the most interactive of all.

INTERFACE

A means of communicating between two different items. For example, a computer and a person interface through a monitor, keyboard, and mouse.

INTERLACED

A low-cost computer screen that is hard on your eyes. An interlaced screen is fine for looking at big, moving pictures, but not for reading text or looking at detailed graphics. See also NON-INTERLACED.

INTERNAL

A device inside your computer, like a built-in CD-ROM drive or modem. Internal units cost less than external units, but are less versatile because they cannot be used with other computers.

INTERNET

The biggest computer network in the world, reaching millions of people, on thousands of interconnected networks. The Internet has a staggering amount of information you can access with a modem from your home, office, or school. No one person or group controls the Internet, so finding a particular piece of information can be challenging.

jmaran@xyzcorp.com

INTERNET ADDRESS

Defines the location of an electronic mailbox on the Internet. An Internet address appears as: yourname@yourlocation. The words following the @ are the machine name and zone. They replace the postal address on an envelope. For example, **jmaran**'s mailbox is on the **xyzcorp** machine that belongs to a **com**mercial zone. See also ZONE.

INTERNET RELAY CHAT (IRC)

"Lounges" on the Internet where people can join and chat (by typing) with others around the world. Each IRC lounge is called a channel and is devoted to a single topic, from poker to Russian culture. Channels can have more than 10 people chatting at one time, and are used by some companies to save on long distance charges.

IP (INTERNET PROTOCOL)

See TCP/IP.

ISA (INDUSTRY STANDARD ARCHITECTURE) BUS

A name for the electronic path (or bus) between a computer's CPU (or brain) and its low speed devices, such as a modem and speakers. High speed devices such as a hard drive use the faster and more expensive PCI bus or VL-Bus. See also PCI BUS and VL-BUS.

ISDN (INTEGRATED SERVICES DIGITAL NETWORK)

A standard for transmitting data over digital telephone lines. It is two to four times faster than the highest speed modem. These lines are often used on the Internet's World Wide Web to quickly transfer or receive text, graphics, sound, and video. ISDN lines are offered by many telephone companies, and their cost is dropping rapidly. See also WORLD WIDE WEB.

ISO (INTERNATIONAL STANDARDS ORGANIZATION)

An international group of experts that sets world standards for technology. Each standard has a unique number. For example, ISO 9660 is a CD-ROM standard that most manufacturers follow. This guarantees that CD-ROM discs made by different manufacturers will work in any CD-ROM drive.

STANDARDS
ISO 1234
ISO 2345
ISO 3456
ISO 4567
ISO 5678
ISO 6789

JEWEL BOX

The plastic case that CD-ROMs and music CDs come in. Just don't try to keep your jewelry in one — it won't fit.

JOYSTICK

A device you can plug into your computer to control the movement of objects, such as a car or plane, in many games. Better control of objects on the screen makes games more realistic.

ORIGINAL

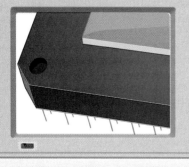

JPEG

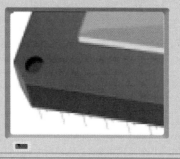

JPEG (JOINT PHOTOGRAPHIC EXPERTS GROUP)

A standard for shrinking graphics so they transmit faster between modems and take up less space on your hard drive. Graphics can be reduced to 5 percent of their original size, but the image quality deteriorates. Compressing graphics to 30 or 40 percent of their original size results in minimal loss of quality.

Ultimately the trade-off between quality and compression depends on the type of graphic. For example, if the graphic contains large areas of an identical color (like a blue sky), then higher compression is possible while still maintaining acceptable quality. See also LOSSY COMPRESSION.

JUSTIFICATION

See ALIGNMENT.

KEY WORD

A word you use to find a word or series of words in a document. For example, if you use the key word "tax", the computer will find all the places in your document where the word "tax" appears.

TAX

Income TAX
TAX Deduction
TAX Planning
Property TAX
TAX Return
TAX Credits

KEYBOARD SHORTCUT

One or more keys you press to do a certain task, instead of picking a menu option with your mouse. Keyboard shortcuts appear next to the commands in a menu. A popular keyboard shortcut to quickly save a file in Windows is Ctrl+S.

KEYPAD

See NUMERIC KEYPAD.

KILOBYTE (K)

See MEMORY CAPACITY.

KIOSK

A computerized information desk. For example, kiosks are often found in airports, giving tourists an overview of the city's attractions. Kiosks offer information interactively via computer screens. To communicate with most kiosks, you use a keyboard and/or a touch-sensitive screen.

LABEL A FLOPPY DISK

To give a name to a floppy disk. This enables you to quickly identify the contents of the disk.

LAN (LOCAL AREA NETWORK)

Several PCs connected together so they can share files and computer equipment, as well as exchange e-mail. Local area networks are usually confined to a small geographic area, such as an office or building.

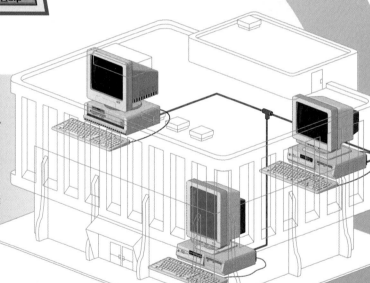

LANDSCAPE

A page turned so that it's wider than it is high. You usually have two choices for printing: landscape and the opposite, portrait. See also PORTRAIT.

L

LAPTOP COMPUTER

A portable computer that weighs between 8 and 10 pounds. Laptops are now obsolete, since the lighter, full-featured notebook computers are widely available.

LASER PRINTER

A high-speed printer that uses a laser beam to form images on a page.

You can buy either a black-and-white or color laser printer.

A laser printer works like a photocopier to produce high-quality printouts.

Most laser printers produce images at 300 dots per inch (dpi). Newer laser printers produce images at 600 dpi or higher. See also DPI.

A laser printer is ideal for routine business and personal documents and for proofing professional graphics work.

Common laser printer speeds include 4, 8, and 12 pages per minute (ppm).

LAUNCH

To start a program. For example, you can launch Word 6.0 for Windows from the Program Manager in Windows 3.1.

LCD (LIQUID CRYSTAL DISPLAY)

The type of screen used in portable computers. This is the same type of display used in most digital wristwatches. LCD screens use less power and are much lighter than the screens used for desktop computers.

LEADER

A line of dots or dashes that leads your eye across a page to related information, especially in a table of contents or index. Also called dot leaders.

LED (LIGHT-EMITTING DIODE)

A small indicator light most often used to show the power is on or the device is being used. LEDs are found on your computer case, monitor, printer, modem, CD-ROM drive, and hard drive.

LEGEND

In a chart or map, a little box that explains the colors or patterns used for different items. Also, Bill Gates of Microsoft, who's gone from a college dropout to one of the richest men in the world.

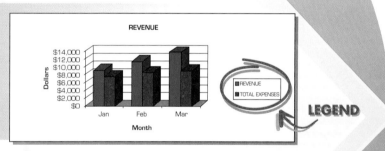

LINE SPACING

Single line spacing

1.5 line spacing

Double line spacing

The amount of space that appears between the lines of text in a document. Most word processors allow you to adjust the line spacing in your document. Common line spacing includes single, 1.5, and double.

LINKING

See OBJECT LINKING AND EMBEDDING.

LITHIUM-ION BATTERY

The longest-lasting (4 to 5 hours) but most expensive type of battery used in portable computers. They take longer to recharge than nickel metal hydride batteries, but you don't have to drain the battery completely before recharging. See also NICKEL CADMIUM BATTERY and NICKEL METAL HYDRIDE BATTERY.

BATTERY PACK
MODEL NO. PA2349

LITHIUM-ION

LOCAL AREA NETWORK

See LAN.

LOGIN: MARY
PASSWORD:

LOG IN OR LOG ON

To gain access to a computer system, usually by entering your user name (login) and password. Once you are logged in, you can run programs, search databases, or transfer files.

LOCAL BUS

See VL-BUS.

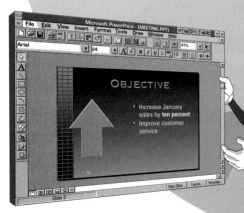

OBJECTIVE

- Increase January sales by ten percent
- Improve customer service

LOOK AND FEEL

The way you interact with a software program: the commands and controls you can use, and how the program looks on the screen. Also called user interface.

LOSSLESS COMPRESSION

A way to shrink a large file into a smaller space without losing information. Lossless compression compacts digital photos and movies so the file takes up less space on your hard drive, but still preserves the details of the original image.

LOSSLESS

ORIGINAL

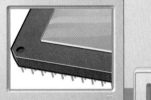

LOSSY

LOSSY COMPRESSION

A way to shrink a large file into a smaller space by eliminating some information. Lossy compression compacts digital photos and movies so the file takes up less space on your hard drive, but it doesn't preserve all the details of the original image. You can compress files more with lossy compression than with lossless compression.

LURKER

Someone who "hangs around" online discussions, reading other people's comments but not contributing. Being a lurker is a good way to check out a newsgroup, but eventually you should contribute something to the discussion.

but by then I wasn't going to be surprised by anything.

Well that's interesting...I'd never have thought he was that kind of person. I always knew he was a great guy, but never in my wildest dream

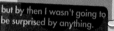

LYCOS

A search tool you can use to find information on any subject on the World Wide Web and the rest of the Internet. Lycos was created at Carnegie Mellon University. Lycos looks through its index of more than 4 million pages to match the key words you enter. To use Lycos, point your Web browser to http://www.lycos.com. If Lycos is busy you can try Yahoo or WebCrawler. See also WEBCRAWLER, WORLD WIDE WEB, and YAHOO.

MACINTOSH

The easy-to-use family of computers introduced by Apple in 1984. Macs were the first well-known machines with a mouse and on-screen windows, menus, and icons. The Mac is still the most popular computer in desktop publishing and multimedia production.

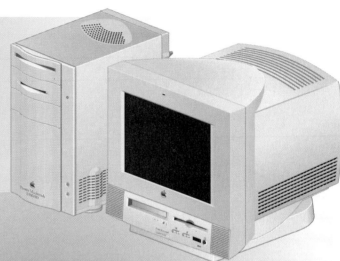

Mr. Johnston	(XXXX)
248 Maple Crescent	(XXXXXXXXX)
Fullerton, CA 92740	(XXXXXXXXX)
Gary Vickers	Please join us at 11 a.m.
27 Willow Avenue	on April 25 for the
Los Angeles, CA 90032	opening of our new office
Jimmy Simpon	building.
19 Water Avenue	
Los Angeles, CA 90048	A buffet lunch will follow.
Mr. Wallace	Yours truly,
17 Duff Crescent	Tim Smiths
Fullerton, CA 92040	
Names	**Form Letter**

MACRO

A small program that automates repetitive tasks requiring multiple steps. A macro allows hard-to-remember tasks to be completed in a single step. It is also a big time saver. Most word processing and spreadsheet programs have a built-in macro program.

MAIL MERGE

A feature in most word processors that lets you produce personalized letters for each person on your mailing list. To do so, you combine a list of names and addresses with a form letter.

MAINFRAME

A computer that stores massive amounts of information. Banks, insurance companies, governments, and research facilities use mainframes to access and process large amounts of data.

MALE CONNECTOR

A computer plug that has pins. An example is a printer cable that you insert into your computer.

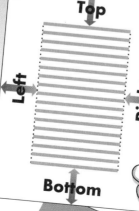

Top

Left

Right

Bottom

MARGIN

The space between text and an edge of a page. Most word processors automatically leave a one-inch margin on all four sides. Most programs let you adjust the margins.

Math Coprocessor – Memory Capacity

MATH COPROCESSOR

A chip that assists the CPU by performing complex math calculations. It can speed up a 386SX or 486SX computer working on heavy-duty spreadsheets or graphics. All DX and Pentium chips have a built-in math coprocessor. Also called a floating point unit (FPU).

MAXIMIZE

To enlarge a window to fill your whole screen. In Windows, you maximize a window by clicking on its Maximize button.

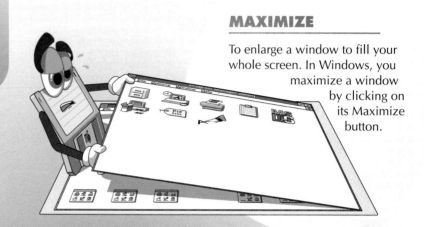

MEGABYTE (MB)

See MEMORY CAPACITY.

CPU	CPU Speed (MHz)	Group and Use
486SX	33MHz	*ECONOMY* word processing, electronic mail
486DX	33MHz	
486DX2	50MHz	*BUSINESS and MULTIMEDIA* word processing, spreadsheet, multimedia, database
486DX2	66MHz	
486DX4	75MHz	
486DX4	100MHz	
PENTIUM	60MHz	
PENTIUM	66MHz	
PENTIUM	75MHz	*POWER USER* desktop publishing, scientific analysis, computer-aided design (CAD)
PENTIUM	90MHz	
PENTIUM	100MHz	
PENTIUM	120MHz	

MEGAHERTZ (MHz)

One million cycles per second — used to measure the speed of a CPU chip. Different chips run at different speeds, as shown in the chart.

As you move down the chart, CPU performance and cost both increase.

Your final decision should be based on your budget and intended use. See also HERTZ.

MEMORY

See RAM.

MEMORY CAPACITY

The amount of information a computer can store in memory. Bytes are used to measure both computer memory (RAM) and the storage capacity of floppy disks, CD-ROM drives, and hard drives.

LIBRARY

BYTE

One character. A character can be a number, letter or symbol.

Note: A byte consists of 8 bits.

KILOBYTE (K)

Approximately one thousand characters, or one page of double spaced text.

GIGABYTE (GB)

Approximately one billion characters, or one thousand novels.

MEGABYTE (MB)

Approximately one million characters, or one novel.

MENU

A list of possible choices, like a menu in a restaurant. For example, from the File menu in Windows 3.1, you can choose such options as copy, move, delete, or exit.

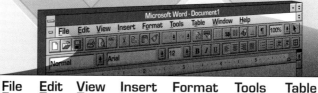

| File | Edit | View | Insert | Format | Tools | Table | Window | Help |

MENU BAR

A strip across the top of a window, listing all the menus available in that program. Don't confuse this with a bar menu, which lists the prices of chicken wings and nachos.

MICROPROCESSOR

See CPU.

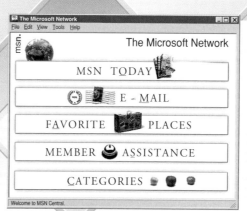

MICROSOFT NETWORK

An online information service launched by Microsoft. The Microsoft Network provides online publications and discussion groups, electronic mail, help with Microsoft products, and access to the Internet.

MIDI (MUSICAL INSTRUMENT DIGITAL INTERFACE)

A set of rules that allow computers, synthesizers, and musical instruments to exchange data. MIDI allows musicians to use a computer to play, record, and edit music. A sound card that supports MIDI ensures that a computer can generate the sounds often found in games, CD-ROMs, and presentation packages.

MIDI SEQUENCER

Software or hardware used by musicians to compose, edit, and play back MIDI files. With a MIDI sequencer you might just become the world's next Mozart.

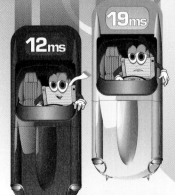

MILLISECOND

Milli is the metric word for one thousandth, so a millisecond is one thousandth of a second. The time it takes a CD-ROM or hard drive to find information (access time) is measured in milliseconds (ms).

FINISH

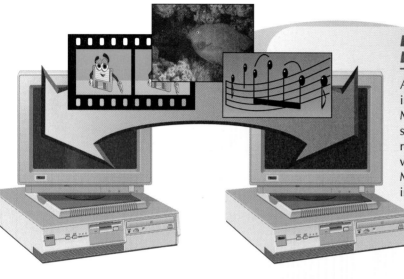

MIME (MULTIPURPOSE INTERNET MAIL EXTENSIONS)

A set of rules that let you send and receive information other than text in e-mail messages. Messages can include text, photographs, programs, sound, and even video. Both the sending and receiving computer must understand MIME to work properly. As more e-mail programs support MIME, sending messages will become more informative and entertaining. See also E-MAIL.

MINIMIZE

To reduce a window to a little picture (icon) on your screen. This helps reduce clutter when you have several windows open at the same time. In Windows, you minimize a window by clicking on its Minimize button.

MIS (MANAGEMENT INFORMATION SYSTEM)

A computer system that receives important business data from all departments in a large company. Then, based on a carefully defined set of rules, the Management Information System generates the information and reports people need to manage the business.

MODEM (MODULATOR-DEMODULATOR)

A device that lets computers communicate through telephone lines.

You can use a modem to exchange e-mail, join a bulletin board system (BBS), use online services like CompuServe, and surf the Internet. The faster your modem, the better.

MODEM SPEEDS AND STANDARDS

Standard	Maximum speed in bits per second (bps)
V.22 bis	2,400
V.32	9,600
V.32 bis	14,400
V.32 terbo	*This is an unofficial standard that may be difficult to upgrade to V.34* 19,200
V.32 FC	*This is an unofficial standard that may be difficult to upgrade to V.34* 28,800
V.34	28,800

The speed that a modem can transmit data through telephone lines is the most important consideration when buying a modem.

Modem standards ensure that modems made by different manufacturers can communicate with each other.

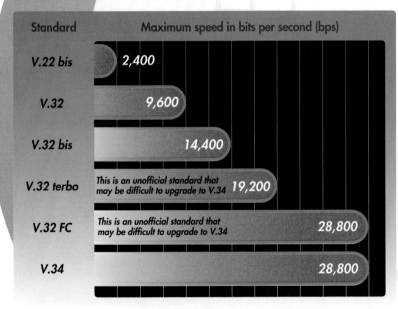

Faster modems cost more, but will save you time and money in the long run. When transferring files, faster modems take less time and save you money on long distance and online service charges.

Modems must use the same speed when exchanging data. A fast modem can talk to a slower modem, but they will communicate at the slower speed.

MONITOR

A device that displays text and graphics generated by a computer. See also COLOR DEPTH, DOT PITCH, NON-INTERLACED, REFRESH RATE, and RESOLUTION (MONITOR).

MORPHING

A gradual transformation from one image into another. For example, some graphics programs can morph a picture of a real mouse into a computer mouse.

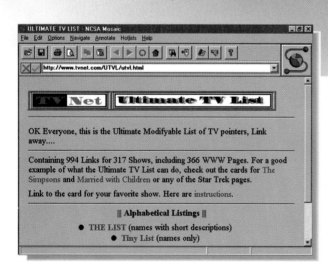

MOSAIC

The first "browser" for the Internet's World Wide Web. Mosaic allows you to visit individual and company "home pages." These pages can display text, graphics, photos, and even links to audio and video clips. In addition, specially underlined text can transport you to other related pages or to other Web sites around the world. See also BROWSER, HOME PAGE, and WORLD WIDE WEB.

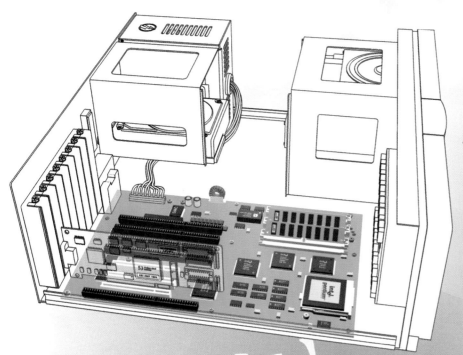

M

MOTHERBOARD

The main circuit board inside a computer. The motherboard contains the CPU chip, memory chips, expansion slots, and other electronic components.

MOUSE

A hand-held device you move on your desk to point to and select items on your screen. When you move the mouse, the mouse pointer on the screen moves in the same direction.

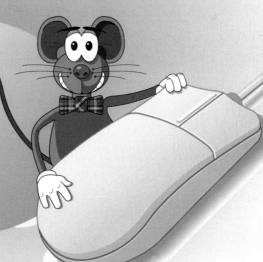

MOUSE POINTER

The little symbol on your screen that you move with your mouse. You use the mouse pointer to point to and select items on your screen. The mouse pointer changes shape, depending on its location on your screen and the action you are performing.

MPC2

The Multimedia Personal Computer (MPC) Marketing Council lists requirements for multimedia computer systems. Certified products display the MPC2 symbol; however, the council's standards are generally low. If you want better multimedia results, purchase a 66MHz 486DX2 or higher computer that has 8MB of RAM and a 540MB hard drive. The CD-ROM drive should be double-speed with 280ms or less access time. It is also recommended you have a 16-bit sound card and a video adapter that supports 16-bit color.

MPEG (MOTION PICTURES EXPERTS GROUP)

See CODEC and FULL-MOTION, FULL-SCREEN VIDEO.

MPR II (SWEDISH LOW-EMISSION STANDARDS)

All monitors, except the screens used in portable computers, emit electromagnetic radiation (EMR). You can protect yourself from the potentially harmful effects by buying a monitor that meets the MPR II guidelines. These guidelines define acceptable levels of EMR.

MS-DOS (MICROSOFT DISK OPERATING SYSTEM)

An older operating system you use by entering text commands. MS-DOS is harder to use than Windows, where you can simply point to and click items on a screen.

MTBF (MEAN TIME BETWEEN FAILURES)

Every computer component, such as a hard drive, will eventually break down. An MTBF figure gives an estimate of a component's life expectancy. The higher the MTBF, the longer the component should last.

M

MULTIMEDIA

A powerful blend of text, graphics, sound, animation, and video on your computer. Multimedia is an effective way of communicating information. Multimedia is used in games, business presentations, interactive tutorials, and information kiosks.

MULTISYNC MONITOR

A monitor that can display images at various resolutions. The higher the resolution, the more information on your screen, but the smaller everything appears.

MULTITASKING

The ability of an operating system to run more than one program at a time. In this example, both WordPad and Paint are multitasking in Windows 95. This makes it very easy to switch between programs or copy text or graphics from one to the other. Windows 3.1, Windows 95, and OS/2 Warp all provide multitasking capabilities.

NETIQUETTE

A code of behavior followed on the Internet when using electronic mail or participating in online discussion groups. As a rule of thumb, don't send anything you'd be embarrassed to show your mother.

NETSCAPE

The most popular "browser" available to surf the World Wide Web on the Internet. Netscape allows you to access Web pages containing text, graphics, sound, and even video from around the world. See also BROWSER, INTERNET, and WORLD WIDE WEB.

NETWORK

A group of connected computers that allows people to share information and equipment. There are two types of networks: local area network (LAN) and wide area network (WAN). See also LAN and WAN.

NETWORK ADAPTER

An expansion card that enables you to connect your PC to a network. You need a network adapter to hook up to an Ethernet or Token-Ring network. You don't need a network adapter to join an online service like CompuServe, which you dial up using a modem. See also EXPANSION CARD.

NETWORK ADMINISTRATOR

A technical expert who is responsible for overseeing a computer network. This can include restoring the network if it goes down, installing software, checking for viruses, making backups, and answering questions. It's a full-time job!

NETWORK SERVER

See
FILE SERVER.

NEWBIE

A beginner on a network, usually the Internet. The online universe is so vast that newbies often get lost and need help from more experienced users.

NEWSGROUP

A discussion group on the Internet dedicated to one topic. Newsgroup members can post messages, have conversations, and send e-mail messages to one another or the group. Thousands of newsgroups exist, on every subject imaginable.

NICKEL CADMIUM (NiCd) BATTERY

The oldest and least expensive type of battery used for portable computers. They last 1 to 2 hours, but suffer from memory effects. This means you must completely drain the battery before recharging it to get the maximum charge. Nickel cadmium batteries are also highly toxic. See also LITHIUM-ION BATTERY and NICKEL METAL HYDRIDE BATTERY.

NICKEL METAL HYDRIDE (NiMH) BATTERY

A type of battery that has almost completely replaced the NiCd battery in portable computers. These batteries last 2 to 3 hours and are less toxic but more expensive than NiCd batteries. NiMH batteries are less prone to memory effects, which means you don't have to completely drain the battery before recharging. See also LITHIUM-ION BATTERY and NICKEL CADMIUM BATTERY.

NOISE

An interference that disrupts the communication between devices, such as two modems. Noise can come from heavy machinery, nearby TVs and radios, or from power lines. To overcome noise, your modem software uses error correction. See also ERROR CORRECTION.

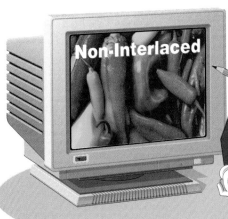

NON-INTERLACED

A type of monitor that decreases the amount of screen flicker to reduce eye strain. Non-interlaced monitors cost more than the old interlaced monitors. See also INTERLACED.

NOTEBOOK COMPUTER

A type of portable computer that weighs between six and eight pounds and is the size of a three-ring binder. A notebook computer can perform the same functions as all but the high-end desktop computers.

NUMERIC KEYPAD

A section of a keyboard, set up like an adding machine or calculator. This allows you to enter numbers and equations quickly into your computer. You can also switch the function of the numeric keypad to use the ↑, ↓, ←, and → keys to move the cursor. See also NUMLOCK KEY.

NUMLOCK KEY

The key you press to switch the function of the numeric keypad between entering numbers and moving the cursor. See also NUMERIC KEYPAD.

Object Linking and Embedding

OBJECT LINKING AND EMBEDDING (OLE)

In Windows, a way to create documents containing objects from other programs. For example, you can place a chart from Excel and a slide from PowerPoint into a Word document.

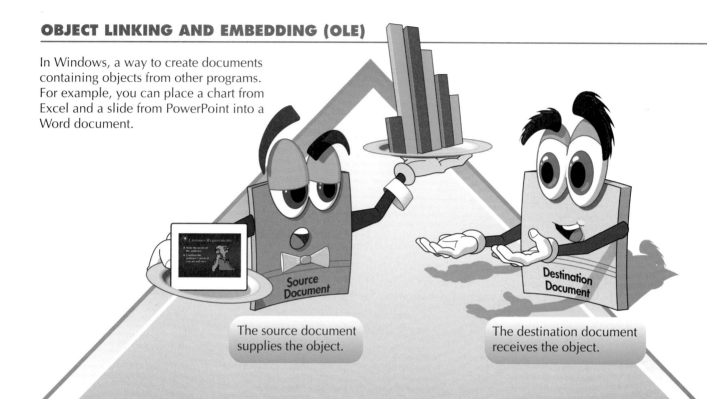

The source document supplies the object.

The destination document receives the object.

EMBEDDING

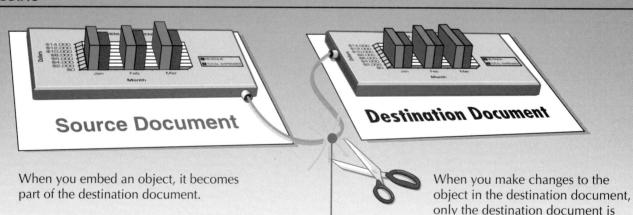

Source Document

Destination Document

When you embed an object, it becomes part of the destination document.

When you make changes to the object in the destination document, only the destination document is affected.

The source document is no longer needed after you embed an object, since the destination document now contains the object.

OBJECT

The information you transfer between programs is called an object. An object can include items such as a picture, chart, text, slide, sound, or video clip.

LINKING

When you link an object, the destination document receives a "screen image" of the object. The object remains in the source document.

Linking objects is useful if you want your destination documents to always contain the most up-to-date information. For example, you can link sales data to a monthly report given to all sales managers. When the sales data changes, all linked reports automatically display the change.

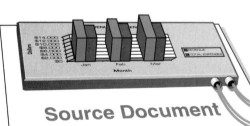

When you link an object, a connection is formed between the source and destination documents.

To make changes to the linked object, you must keep a copy of the source document. Changes you make to the source document affect all destination documents.

OCR (OPTICAL CHARACTER RECOGNITION)

Software that can read handwritten or printed text. OCR software interprets the lines and squiggles on a page and converts them into characters. This provides a quick way to enter text into your computer. OCR software is commonly used with scanners.

Phew

OFF-SITE STORAGE

Storing a copy of important files in a separate location. This provides an extra copy of your files just in case your house burns down or your computer is stolen.

ONLINE

Plugged in and ready for action. Online describes two devices connected by a telephone or computer cable that are ready and able to communicate. For example, your computer is online when you dial another computer with your modem and make a connection.

ONLINE SERVICE

A computer network you dial up with your computer and modem. Members of an online service can exchange electronic mail, collect research, order products and play games. Most online services have a basic charge per month plus added charges for certain features. Two popular online services are CompuServe and America Online.

ON-SITE SERVICE

A computer fix-it service that does house calls. This saves you from having to bring your computer to the store, or worse — shipping it back to the factory.

OPERATING SYSTEM

The master control program that works like a traffic cop to direct traffic and keep everything flowing smoothly inside your computer. Two popular operating systems are Windows and OS/2.

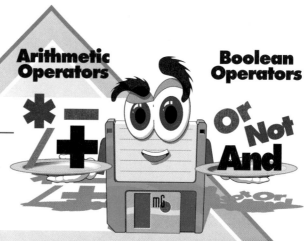

OPERATOR

A mathematical symbol used in a spreadsheet formula, such as +, -, *, or /. Also, a term used to search for information in a database, such as And, Or, or Not. See also BOOLEAN LOGIC.

Arithmetic Operators

Boolean Operators

OPTIMIZE

To tune up your computer so everything is in tip-top shape. For example, optimizing your hard disk includes running a maintenance check, scanning it for viruses, and defragmenting your hard disk. See also ANTI-VIRUS SOFTWARE and DEFRAGMENT.

ORIENTATION

See LANDSCAPE and PORTRAIT.

OS/2 WARP

The latest PC operating system from IBM. OS/2 Warp provides a graphical user interface and can run programs written for MS-DOS and Windows. Some people say OS/2 is technically superior to Windows, but OS/2 has only sold 1/10th the copies.

OUTLINE FONT

A type style in which each character's outline is stored as a formula, rather than a pattern of dots (bitmap). It is also called a scalable font because the outline can be scaled up or down to print at any size. See also BITMAPPED FONT.

OUTPUT DEVICE

A device that lets a computer communicate with you, such as a monitor, printer, or a set of speakers.

OVERDRIVE CPU

A CPU chip that replaces an existing CPU chip to increase the processing power of a computer. When you use an OverDrive CPU, you do not have to upgrade other parts of the computer to see an improvement in performance.

Not all CPUs can be upgraded. Even if you can upgrade your old CPU, the rest of your computer may not be modern enough to make it worthwhile. In many situations, your best choice is to buy a new computer. See also CPU.

P6

See
686 CHIP.

PAGE BREAK

Where one page ends and another begins
in a document. You can have your word
processor automatically insert a page
break or you can manually insert your
own. A page break appears as a
dashed line across your
screen.

PAINT PROGRAM

Software used to create images that simulate
watercolor paintings or enhance scanned pictures
or graphics. A paint program gives you control
over the exact color and shading of every dot
(pixel) on the screen, but images cannot
be as easily resized as they can in draw
programs. Two popular paint programs are
PC Paintbrush and Windows Paint. See
also DRAW PROGRAM.

PALETTE

A collection of tools organized
in their own window. Each tool is
represented by a graphic. For example,
in a paint program, you can select a tool
from a palette to draw wavy lines.

PALETTE

P

PARALLEL PORT

See PORT.

PASSIVE MATRIX SCREEN

A type of screen used in portable computers that is not as bright as an active matrix screen, but uses less power and is not as expensive. See also ACTIVE MATRIX SCREEN.

PASSWORD

A secret code you type into a computer system to prove you are who you say you are, much like the number you use to access your account at a bank machine. The best password is one that combines letters, symbols, and numbers, like *black1.

PASTE

To insert the last information you cut or copied into a document. You can use cut and paste to move information within or between documents. See also COPY and CUT.

PATH

The exact directions to a file on your
computer. For example, to find the file
"MERGE.LET", the path consists of three
parts: a letter for the drive (e.g., C),
a name for the folder (e.g., DATA),
and a name for the file (e.g., MERGE.LET).
The complete path is C:\DATA\MERGE.LET.

PC CARD

A lightweight, credit card sized device that lets you add
a new feature to a portable computer. Without PC
Cards, adding features to a portable computer would
not only weigh it down, but also take up valuable
space. PC Cards can provide modem and
networking capabilities, additional
hard drive space, and CD-quality
sound. Also called a PCMCIA Card.

PCI (PERIPHERAL COMPONENT INTERCONNECT) BUS

An electronic path (or bus) between
a computer's microprocessor (or brain) and
its devices, such as a monitor or hard
drive. The PCI bus is used in
Pentium computers and
operates at the same speed as
the VL-Bus, but can connect
more devices. The PCI bus also
supports Plug and Play. See also ISA
BUS, PLUG AND PLAY, and VL-BUS.

PCL (PRINTER CONTROL LANGUAGE)

Software that tells your
printer how to print a page.
Almost all IBM compatible
laser printers support PCL.
PCL translates text and
graphics into codes your
printer understands. PCL is
ideal for routine office tasks
and it is cheaper than its
less-common alternative,
PostScript. See also
POSTSCRIPT.

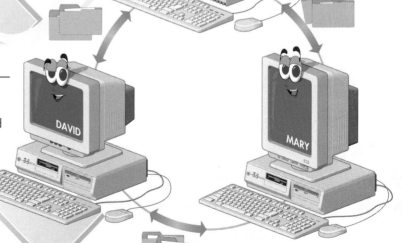

P

PCMCIA

See PC CARD.

PDA (PERSONAL DIGITAL ASSISTANT)

A pocket-sized computer that is designed to do specific tasks. PDAs typically include software to store phone numbers, appointments, and "to-do" lists. You use a special pen to input and access your information. PDAs can also contain a wireless fax modem. One of the most well-known PDAs is Apple's Newton.

PDA (KEYBOARD-ENHANCED)

A pocket-sized computer that is designed to do specific tasks. Keyboard-enhanced PDAs include software to store phone numbers, appointments, and "to-do" lists. You use a keyboard and a special pen to input and access your information. Some keyboard-enhanced PDAs accept PC Cards to expand memory or communications. See also PC CARD and PDA.

PEER-TO-PEER NETWORK

An efficient way to connect less than 10 computers. In a peer-to-peer network, each computer can access the files stored on any other computer. Two popular peer-to-peer networks are Artisoft's LANtastic and Microsoft's Windows for Workgroups.

PENTIUM

The preferred chip for Windows computers today, due to its high speed and performance. Produced by Intel, the Pentium processes information twice as fast as the 486 chip it replaces. If you're shopping for a PC and can afford it, buy a computer with a Pentium CPU. See also 586 CHIP and CPU.

PERIPHERAL

Any external device that plugs into your computer, such as a printer, modem, scanner, or tape drive.

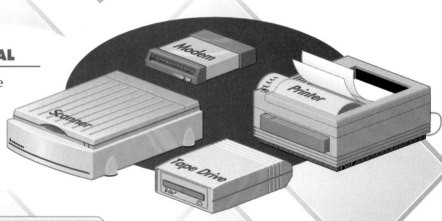

PERSONAL DIGITAL ASSISTANT

See PDA.

PHOTO CD

A system from Kodak that transfers 35mm slides or negatives onto a CD-ROM disc. The CD-ROM can hold 100 photographs. To display the images, your CD-ROM drive must conform to the CD-ROM XA standard.

P

PIRACY

Unauthorized copying of software for personal use or distribution. Some software manufacturers use schemes like copy protection to guard against this activity. Pirating software is breaking the law and could land the offender in jail.

PIXEL

The display on a monitor is made up of a collection of dots called pixels. For monochrome screens, a pixel contains one dot. For color displays, a pixel contains three dots (red, green, and blue). By varying the intensity of the dots, you can display up to 256 shades of gray or millions of colors. Pixel stands for picture element.

PKZIP

See
ZIPPED
FILE.

Platform – Pop-Up Menu

PLATFORM

A family of computers sharing the same CPU or microprocessor family. Software written for one platform will not work on another platform. For example, Microsoft Excel for Windows will not operate on a Macintosh computer.

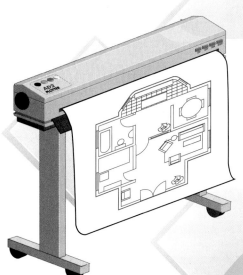

PLOTTER

A large printer that generates high-quality documents by moving ink pens over the surface of a page. Plotters are particularly useful to engineers and architects, as they produce high-quality blueprints, maps, and floor plans. Also called an X-Y plotter.

PLUG AND PLAY

The ability to add new features to a computer and immediately use them. Plug and Play eliminates complicated installation procedures. Macintosh equipment has always been plug and play, and now Windows 95 is trying to help PCs become just as simple.

P

POINT SIZE

The size of the characters on your screen or printout, given in points. There are approximately 72 points in an inch. The larger the point size, the larger the characters. Most business letters are usually printed at 10 or 12 points. Also called font size.

10 point
12 point
14 point
18 point
24 point

POINTER

See
MOUSE
POINTER.

POINTING STICK

A control, resembling a pencil eraser, that replaces the mouse on a portable computer. You push the pointing stick with your finger to move the mouse pointer around the screen. In a confined space, a lot of people find a pointing stick more convenient than a mouse.

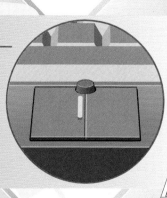

POP-UP MENU

A list of options that appears on the screen when you click the right mouse button. Pop-up menus are common in Windows 3.1 and Windows 95 programs. The options in the pop-up menu refer to the selected area on the screen.

PORT

A socket at the back of a computer where you plug in an external device. This lets instructions and data flow between the computer and the device.

SERIAL PORT

A serial port has either 9 or 25 pins. This type of port connects a mouse, modem, scanner, or occasionally a printer. Also called a male connector.

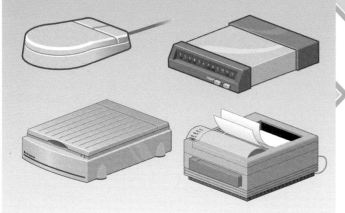

A serial port sends one bit of data, or one-eighth of a character, through a cable at a time. Serial ports can reliably send information more than 20 feet.

A cable that plugs into a serial port has either 9 or 25 holes.

MOUSE PORT

A mouse port connects a mouse.

KEYBOARD PORT

A keyboard port connects a keyboard.

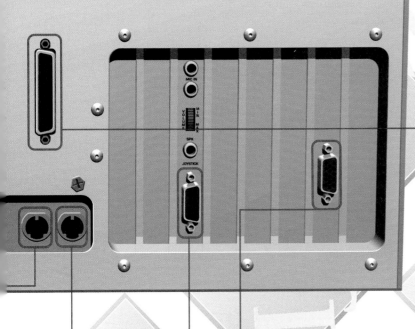

PARALLEL PORT

A parallel port has 25 holes. This type of port connects a printer or tape drive. Also called a female connector.

A parallel port is faster than a serial port. It sends 8 bits of data, or one character, through a cable at a time. Parallel ports cannot reliably send information more than 20 feet.

A cable that plugs into a parallel port has 25 pins.

GAME PORT

A game port connects a joystick.

MONITOR PORT

A monitor port connects a monitor.

PORT REPLICATOR

A device with the same ports as those found on the back of your portable computer. You plug the equipment on your desk — monitor, printer, modem, and so on — into the port replicator. Then you can connect your portable to the port replicator in one step, and use all the devices on your desk without having to attach each one individually.

PORTABLE COMPUTER

Any computer small and light enough to carry with you. There are several categories of portables, from laptops that weigh about 10 pounds and are the size of a telephone book, to palmtops that weigh less than one pound and are small enough to slip in a coat pocket.

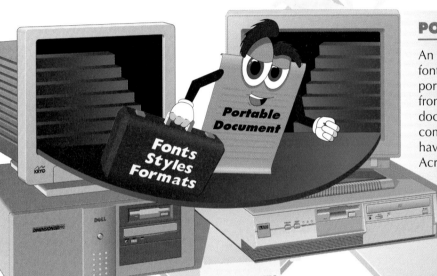

PORTABLE DOCUMENT

An electronic document that carries its fonts, styles, and formatting. Using special portable document software (e.g., Acrobat from Adobe), you can create a portable document, and then send it to another computer. The receiving computer must have special "viewing" software (e.g., Acrobat Viewer) to display and print the document. However, the viewer software does not allow the document to be edited.

PORTRAIT

A page turned so that it's higher than it is wide. You usually have two choices for printing: portrait and the opposite, landscape. See also LANDSCAPE.

POSTSCRIPT

Software that tells your printer how to print a page. PostScript translates text and graphics into codes your printer understands. It is popular in the graphic arts industry and is more expensive than its more common alternative, PCL. See also PCL.

POWER SUPPLY

Every computer has a power supply to change the electricity from the wall outlet into electricity the computer can use. The capacity of a power supply is measured in watts. A typical computer requires 200 watts to operate. This isn't very much, when you consider that an average hair dryer uses seven times as much power.

PPM (PAGES PER MINUTE)

A measure of how many pages a printer can print in a minute. In a busy office environment a printer with a high PPM is recommended.

PPP (POINT-TO-POINT PROTOCOL)

A method of connecting your computer and modem directly to the Internet so that you can use features such as the World Wide Web and electronic mail. PPP is faster than SLIP, which it is gradually replacing. Many Internet companies offer SLIP or PPP connections to the Internet. See also PROTOCOL and SLIP.

PREVIEW

A feature in most programs that shows you on the screen how your document will look when printed. Preview lets you view the overall look of the page, including margins, line spacing, page numbers, and other details. This ensures you'll get what you expect.

PRINT BUFFER/PRINT SPOOLER

A computer can send data faster than a printer can accept and process the data. A print spooler or print buffer acts like a dam, holding the data and then releasing it at a speed the printer can handle.

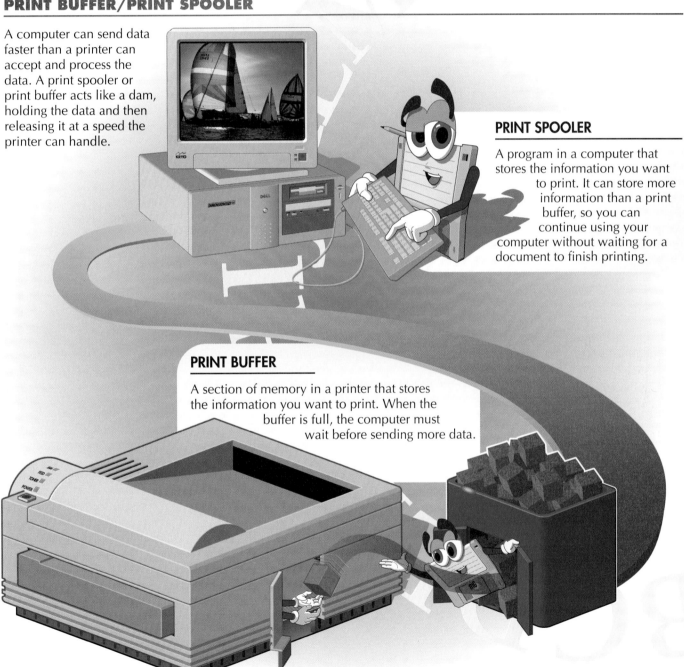

PRINT SPOOLER

A program in a computer that stores the information you want to print. It can store more information than a print buffer, so you can continue using your computer without waiting for a document to finish printing.

PRINT BUFFER

A section of memory in a printer that stores the information you want to print. When the buffer is full, the computer must wait before sending more data.

PRINTER

A device that produces a paper copy of the information on your screen. You can use a printer to produce letters, invoices, newsletters, reports, labels, and much more. See also DOT MATRIX PRINTER, INK JET PRINTER, and LASER PRINTER.

PRINTER DRIVER

Software that helps a printer communicate with your computer. If you buy a new printer you will need to install a new printer driver.

PRODIGY

An online information service you can dial up with your modem for a monthly fee. Members of Prodigy can exchange e-mail, join discussion groups, and play computer games. Owned by IBM and Sears, Prodigy is best known as an electronic shopping mall where you can order products. See also ONLINE SERVICE.

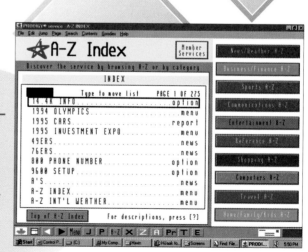

P

PROGRAM

See
APPLICATION
SOFTWARE.

PROTOCOL

A set of rules for how two computers speak
to one another through a modem or
network. This ensures that the
message gets through OK. Both
the sender and receiver must
use the same protocol. Two
popular modem protocols
are Xmodem and Zmodem.

PUBLIC DOMAIN

Software written as a good
deed by some kind-hearted
programmer, and then donated
to the public. Anyone can
use and copy public domain
software free of charge,
but it is not always
as well-written or
tested as commercial
software.

PULL-DOWN MENU

A list of options that is revealed when
you select a menu name at the top of
a window. For example, the File menu
in Excel 5 for Windows is a pull-down
menu. Also called a menu.

QIC (QUARTER-INCH CARTRIDGE) DRIVE

A device used to back up information stored on a single computer. A QIC drive stores data on cartridges. QIC-80 is currently the most popular cartridge. See also DAT DRIVE.

QUAD-SPEED DRIVE

A CD-ROM drive that reads information four times as fast as a single-speed CD-ROM drive. Quad-speed drives are more expensive than single- and double-speed drives, but the high speed results in better performance, especially when viewing multimedia presentations.

QUERY

To ask for selected information from a database. For example, you could query a database of baseball statistics to find all the players who batted more than .250 in the last 10 games.

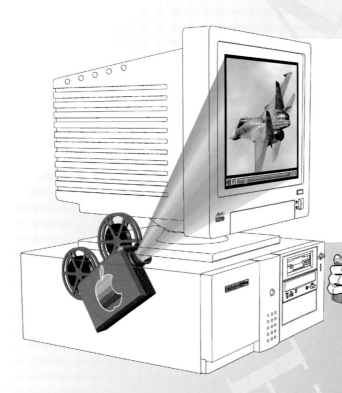

Q

QUICKTIME

Software from Apple that adds multimedia sound and video capabilities to both Macintosh and Windows PCs. QuickTime is a toolbox of software programs that helps multimedia publishers create movies, animation, and sound. A QuickTime movie is a video you can watch on your computer screen.

QWERTY KEYBOARD

A standard keyboard named after the first six letters in the top row. This keyboard was actually designed to slow down typists who kept jamming the early mechanical typewriters. Now everyone still uses the less-efficient QWERTY keyboards because, as the saying goes, it is hard to teach an old dog new tricks. See also DVORAK KEYBOARD.

RADIO BUTTON

Shut down

You would like to:
...n the computer
...computer?
...programs and log...

A little round button you can click in a dialog box to select one of several choices. You can select only one radio button at a time. When you select another button, the original button is deselected.

RAM CACHE

See CACHE (RAM).

RAM (RANDOM ACCESS MEMORY)

Electronic memory that temporarily stores information inside a computer. See also STORAGE CAPACITY.

$$3.\text{?}4 \times (3a^2 \times 700) \div 1,298 - .654$$
$$8\text{?} \text{?} \times \frac{6.78}{2309}$$
$$6b \div 98$$

Memory works like a blackboard that is constantly overwritten with new data.

The amount of memory, or memory size, in a computer determines the number of programs you can run at once. Memory size also determines how fast your programs will operate.

The data stored in memory is temporary. If you do not save the data, it will disappear when you turn off the computer.

RANDOM ACCESS

The most efficient way of storing and retrieving information. With random access, information is readily available. For example, a music CD has random access — you can immediately skip to your favorite song.

The opposite is sequential access, which stores information in a line, so it is not immediately available. For example, a music tape has sequential access — you have to fast forward or rewind through songs to reach your favorite one.

READ ONLY

Information you can read but not change, like a printed book. A read only file on your computer is a file you can open, read, or print, but not edit.

READ ONLY MEMORY

See ROM.

README FILE

A text file that gives last-minute tips and corrections that didn't make it into the manual for a new software release. You can open README files with most word processors.

Read/Write Head

READ/WRITE HEADS

The tiny parts of a hard or floppy disk drive that transfer information to and from the disk. Read/write heads can be damaged by severe vibrations.

EMPLOYEE INFORMATION

Last Name	First Name	Street	City	State	Zip Code
Smith	John	258 Linton Ave.	New York	NY	10010
Lang	Kristin	50 Tree Lane	Boston	MA	02117
Oram	Derek	68 Cacker Ave.	San Francisco	CA	94110
Gray	Russel	1 Hollywood Blvd.	Cincinnati	OH	45217
Atherley	Peter	47 Cosby Ave.	Las Vegas	NV	89116
Talbot	Mark	26 Arnold Cres.	Jacksonville	FL	
Coleman	Duane	401 Idon Dr.	Nashville		
Sanvido	Dean				

REBOOT

See
BOOT.

RECORD

One complete entry in a database about a person, place, or thing. For example, a record can include the complete address of an employee.

RECOVER

To bring back a file you accidentally deleted. Sometimes you can recover a file you erased by using software such as Delete Sentry in MS-DOS 6.2 or the Recycle Bin in Windows 95. You can also recover a lost or damaged file by restoring it from your latest backup.

REFERENCE

See ABSOLUTE REFERENCE and RELATIVE REFERENCE.

REFORMAT A DISK

To erase all the information from a hard or floppy disk in order to prepare it for use. If your hard disk is not working properly, you may have to reformat it and reinstall all your programs. Always check with a computer expert before reformatting your hard disk. Reformatting is not reversible, so proceed with caution!

REFRESH RATE

Every screen needs to be refreshed many times a second, or it will fade or flicker. The higher your screen's refresh rate, the easier it is on your eyes. Color monitors with a refresh rate above 70 Hertz are considered flicker-free.

RELATIONAL DATABASE

A database containing two or more tables that share common information.

Relational databases are powerful and flexible, but complicated to set up and learn. They are often used for accounting purposes. See also DATABASE and FLAT FILE DATABASE.

Relational databases let you combine data from different tables to create invoices or reports. For example, you can combine order and product information to quickly create an invoice.

If you change data in one table, the data will change in all related tables. This saves you time because you only have to change the data once.

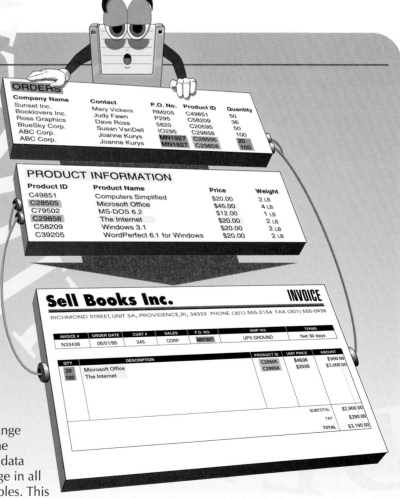

RELATIVE REFERENCE

A reference to a cell in a spreadsheet (e.g., A1). When you copy a formula containing relative references to another cell, the relative references automatically change.

A	A	B	C	D
1	10	20	5	
2	20	30	10	
3	30	40	20	
4	60	90	35	
5				
6				

+A1+A2+A3   →   +B1+B2+B3   +C1+C2+C3

This cell contains the formula +A1+A2+A3

If you copy the formula to other cells in the spreadsheet, the relative references in the new formulas automatically change.

RELEASE NUMBER

The number after the decimal place in a program's number. The release number usually indicates a minor improvement to the program. For example, WordPerfect 6.1 for Windows was released to improve upon WordPerfect 6.0 for Windows. See also VERSION NUMBER.

WordPerfect 6.1
Format Table Graphics T
b i U Aᵇ
Left 1.0

REMOVABLE HARD DISK

A hard disk you can slip out of your computer and take with you. Removable hard disks are handy for backups, and for transferring very large graphics and multimedia files from one location to another. Two popular types of removable hard disks are Bernoulli and SyQuest. See also HARD DISK.

R

RENAME

To change the name of a file, directory (folder), or disk. To rename any of these, you must follow the naming rules for your operating system.

REPETITIVE STRAIN INJURY (RSI)

A condition of numbness, pain, or general fatigue in your fingers, arms, wrists, neck, back, or shoulders. An RSI is caused by a combination of factors, such as high stress, a poorly designed work area, and repetitive movements such as typing. When using a computer, RSIs can be prevented by using wrist supports, an adjustable chair that supports your lower back, and by taking frequent breaks. See also CARPAL TUNNEL SYNDROME and ERGONOMICS.

RESET BUTTON

A button that restarts a computer without turning the power off and then on again. This button is useful when a computer does not respond to your commands.

RESET   POWER

RESOLUTION (MONITOR)

The amount of information a monitor can display. It is measured by the number of dots, called pixels, that a monitor can display horizontally and vertically.

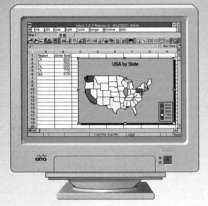

640 X 480 PIXELS

When you use a lower resolution, the images on your screen are larger. This is useful if you have trouble seeing small images.

800 X 600 PIXELS

1,280 X 1,024 PIXELS

When you use a higher resolution, the images on your screen are smaller. This is useful if you want to display more information on your screen.

RESOLUTION (PRINTER)

The quality of the images on a printed page. Resolution is measured in dots per inch (dpi). A higher resolution results in sharper, more detailed images.

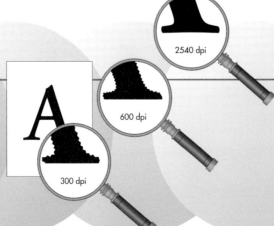

2540 dpi

600 dpi

300 dpi

Generally, a resolution of 300 dpi is acceptable for most office documents, although 600 dpi printers are becoming more popular. If you require over 1200 dpi, you can take your work to a service bureau.

RESOLUTION (SCANNER)

The amount of detail a scanner can detect. A higher resolution results in more detailed scanned images but requires more scanning time and storage space. Resolution is measured in dots per inch (dpi).

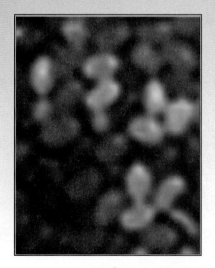

20 dpi

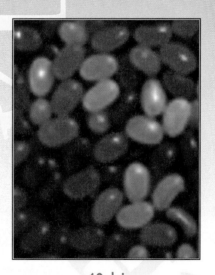

60 dpi

300 dpi

RESTORE

To retrieve a file from your latest backup and copy it to your computer. If you accidentally erase a file, or if a file is damaged, you can restore it from your backup tape or floppy disk.

RJ-11 CONNECTOR

The standard telephone jack you use to plug a phone or modem into a wall outlet. These connectors are standard throughout North America.

ROM (READ ONLY MEMORY)

A type of memory chip that does not lose information, even when the power is turned off. Once data is programmed into the ROM chip, its contents cannot be altered. For example, ROM BIOS chips are used to store information for starting up your computer. ROM chips are also used to store programs for hand-held computers. See also BIOS.

ROOT DIRECTORY

The top level of a hard drive. When you turn on your computer, it automatically accesses the root directory — called C:\. The root directory contains other directories or folders (e.g., DATA), which you can use to store and organize your information. See also DIRECTORY.

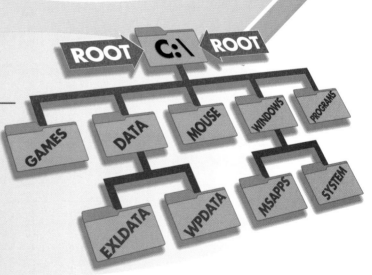

ROUTER

A specialized computer that finds the best way to get an electronic message to its proper destination. Like a good travel agent, a router picks the most efficient route, based on the traffic and the number of stop overs. Any e-mail you send through the Internet is passed through a number of routers.

2			Jan
3		4	
5	REVENUE		8700
6			
7	Payroll		3850

ROW

A horizontal line of boxes in a spreadsheet or table. In a spreadsheet, each row is identified by a number.

RULER

An image of a ruler on your screen in a word processing, desktop publishing, or graphics program. You can use the ruler to position text or graphics on a page. In most programs, you can hide or show the ruler.

File   Edit   View   Insert   Format

Normal   12

Dear Mr. Johnston:

WORD 6.0 FOR WINDOWS™ includes many new and exciting features. A brief presentation of this software is scheduled for next Friday at 11:00 a.m. in the conference room.

Sans Serif Font – Scroll Bar

SANS SERIF FONT

A plain and simple font that has no fancy designs on each character. Generally, sans serif fonts are used for signs, posters, and headlines. Common examples of sans serif fonts are Helvetica and Avant Garde.

The opposite is a serif font, which has fancy designs on each character. Generally, serif fonts are used in newspapers and books. Common examples of serif fonts are Times and Palatino.

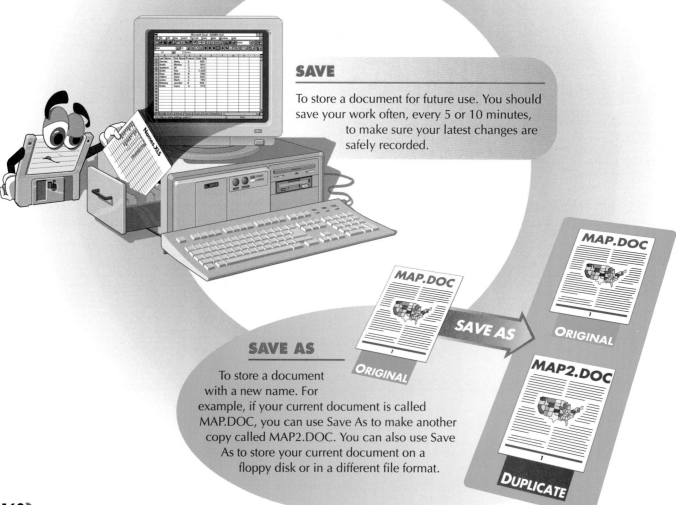

SAVE

To store a document for future use. You should save your work often, every 5 or 10 minutes, to make sure your latest changes are safely recorded.

SAVE AS

To store a document with a new name. For example, if your current document is called MAP.DOC, you can use Save As to make another copy called MAP2.DOC. You can also use Save As to store your current document on a floppy disk or in a different file format.

SCANNER

See
FLATBED SCANNER,
HAND-HELD SCANNER, and
RESOLUTION (SCANNER).

SCREEN SAVER

A moving picture or pattern that appears on the screen when you do not use your computer for a period of time. Screen savers were originally designed to prevent screen burn, which occurs when an image appears in a fixed position for a period of time. Today's monitors are better designed to prevent screen burn, although people still use screen savers for entertainment.

SCREEN

See
MONITOR.

SCROLL

To move through a document. If your document contains a lot of text, your computer screen cannot display all the text at the same time. You can scroll through the document to view the other areas.

SCROLL BAR

A bar at the edge of a window you can use to scroll (move) through a document. By sliding a little box along the scroll bar, you can quickly move up, down, left, or right through your document.

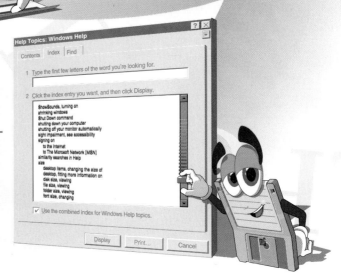

SCSI (SMALL COMPUTER SYSTEM INTERFACE)

A fast and flexible, but more expensive, way to connect a hard drive to a computer. SCSI can also connect other devices such as CD-ROM drives, tape drives, scanners, and printers. High-end computers and network servers come with SCSI.

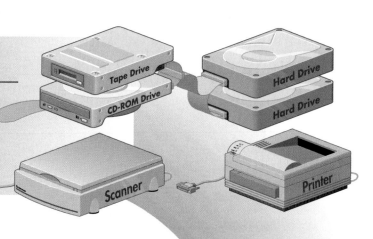

SEARCH

A method of finding information in a document or database. For example, you can search through a document to find every occurrence of the word "CD-ROM". Computers are great for this kind of searching because they never miss a thing.

SEARCH AND REPLACE

To find and change every occurrence of a word or phrase in a document. For example, you can search for every instance of "Jodi" and replace it with "Jody". Search and replace is available in most word processing and desktop publishing software.

S

SECTION

Part of a document that you want to look different from the rest. In each section, you can change items such as the header, footer, and number of columns. Word 6 for Windows enables you to separate your document into sections.

SECURITY (ONLINE)

Nobody wants an unscrupulous hacker to get their credit card number through the Internet. So several groups are working on online security to make it safe to buy and sell online. Using special built-in software called S-HTTP (Secure Hypertext Transfer Protocol) or SSL (Secure Sockets Layer), you'll be able to send payments safely across the Internet.

SELECT TEXT

To highlight text you want to change. For example, you can cut, copy, move, or delete text you have selected.

SEPARATIONS

See COLOR SEPARATION.

SEQUENCER

See MIDI SEQUENCER.

SERIAL PORT

See PORT.

SERIF

See SANS SERIF FONT.

SERVER

See FILE SERVER.

SERVICE BUREAU

A business that provides color printers, separators, scanners, or photocopiers to individuals or businesses for a fee.

SERVICE PROVIDER

A company that connects individuals and businesses to the Internet for a fee. A service provider will give you access to the Internet, normally through a SLIP or PPP connection. Some service providers will also provide you with software or lessons to use the tools on the Internet. Often called ISPs (Internet Service Providers). See also PPP and SLIP.

SHAREWARE

Software you can try before you buy. You can get shareware from a computer store, bulletin board system (BBS), or even a friend. If you find shareware you like, you can pay the developer a small fee and they will send you the latest version. See also BBS.

SHORTCUT

See KEYBOARD SHORTCUT.

S-HTTP

See SECURITY (ONLINE).

SIMM (SINGLE IN-LINE MEMORY MODULE)

A narrow circuit board that contains RAM
(also called DRAM) memory chips. The more
RAM chips you add to the computer, the faster
it operates and the more programs you can
run at the same time.

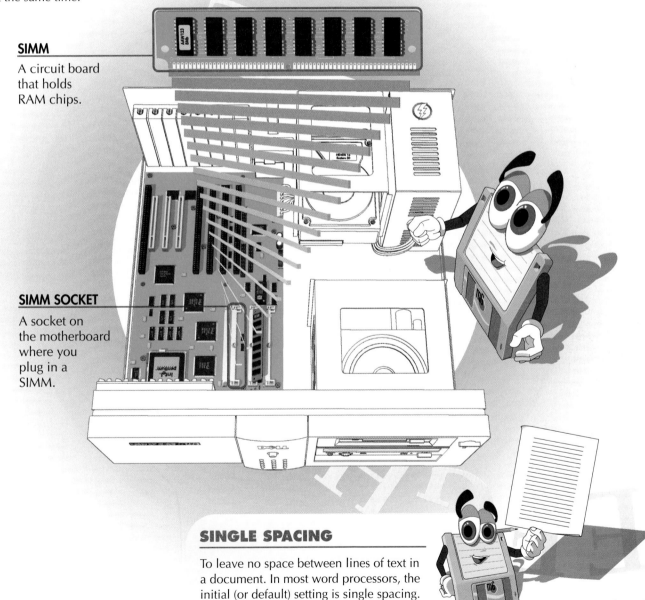

SIMM

A circuit board
that holds
RAM chips.

SIMM SOCKET

A socket on
the motherboard
where you
plug in a
SIMM.

SINGLE SPACING

To leave no space between lines of text in
a document. In most word processors, the
initial (or default) setting is single spacing.

SITE LICENSE

A special license permitting an organization to use software (e.g., WordPerfect, Excel) on multiple computers. A site license is common in large corporations because the overall cost is much less than having to buy the software for each individual computer.

SLIDE SHOW

A combination of text and graphics that are shown one after the other to make sales pitches or illustrate technical presentations. Two popular programs for creating slide shows are Microsoft PowerPoint and Lotus Freelance Graphics.

SLIP (SERIAL LINE INTERNET PROTOCOL)

A method of connecting your computer and modem directly to the Internet so that you can use features such as the World Wide Web and electronic mail. SLIP is being replaced by PPP. Many Internet companies offer SLIP or PPP connections to the Internet. See also PPP and PROTOCOL.

S

SLOT

See
EXPANSION
SLOT.

```
To: Jeff                    12:20am  12.3.95

Glad to see you're back from vacation!  :-)

Too bad you got sunburned on the 1st day  :-(

Fortunately, you can recover over the next year,
for you have no more allotted vacation time left!  ;-)
```

Smile   **Frown**   **Wink**

SMILEY

Symbols used to convey emotions and gestures in messages. Smileys represent human faces if you turn them sideways. Smileys are frequently used when communicating on the Internet. Also called emoticon.

:-)	Smile	:D	Laugh
:-(	Frown	:-O	Surprise
;-)	Wink		

SNAIL MAIL

A name given to the regular postal service by people who use electronic mail. While sending international mail through the postal service can take weeks, with electronic mail it takes seconds.

SOFTWARE

Electronic instructions that tell your computer what to do. Without software, a computer is like an airplane without a pilot. There are two types of software: operating system software and application software.

Operating system software (e.g., MS-DOS, Windows) sets the rules for how computer hardware and application software work together.

Application software (e.g., Word, Lotus 1-2-3) helps you to write letters, analyze numbers, manage finances, draw pictures, and even play games.

Software Suite

SOFTWARE SUITE

A collection of software programs all sold together in one package. Three popular software suites are Lotus SmartSuite, Microsoft Office, and Novell PerfectOffice.

ADVANTAGES

- It costs less to buy programs as part of a suite than to buy them individually.

- Programs look and act the same. Once you learn one program, you can easily learn the others.

- Programs can exchange data and interact in ways they cannot do alone.

DISADVANTAGE

- All the programs come from the same manufacturer. You may not get the best combination of features for your needs.

LOTUS SMARTSUITE

AMI PRO
A word processing program that lets you create documents such as letters, reports, and newsletters.

1-2-3
A spreadsheet program that lets you manage and analyze information.

FREELANCE GRAPHICS
A presentation program that lets you plan, organize, and design presentations.

ORGANIZER
A personal information manager that lets you keep track of appointments and other events.

APPROACH
A database program that lets you manage large collections of information.

MICROSOFT OFFICE

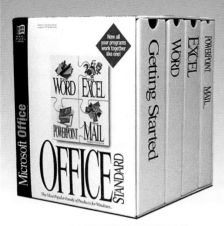

WORD
A word processing program that lets you create documents such as letters, reports, and newsletters.

EXCEL
A spreadsheet program that lets you manage and analyze information.

POWERPOINT
A presentation program that lets you plan, organize, and design presentations.

MAIL
An electronic mail program that lets you exchange messages with other people on a network.

The Professional version of Microsoft Office includes all of these programs, plus Access.

Access is a database program that lets you manage large collections of information.

NOVELL PERFECTOFFICE

WORDPERFECT
A word processing program that lets you create documents such as letters, reports, and newsletters.

QUATTRO PRO
A spreadsheet program that lets you manage and analyze information.

PRESENTATIONS
A presentation program that lets you plan, organize, and design presentations.

INFOCENTRAL
A personal information manager that lets you keep track of appointments and other events.

GROUPWISE
An office manager that includes electronic mail, scheduling, and task management features.

ENVOY
A program that lets other people view a document, even if their computers do not have the program that created the document.

The Professional version of PerfectOffice includes all of these programs, plus Paradox and Visual AppBuilder.

Paradox is a database program that lets you manage large collections of information. Visual AppBuilder is a programming tool that lets you develop applications using visual techniques rather than programming code.

Sort – Split Screen

SORT

To organize a list of information in a different order. For example, you can sort items in alphabetical order (a to z), ascending order (a to z, 1 to 10), or descending order (z to a, 10 to 1). This is a mindless job that computers excel at since it requires speed but no imagination.

SOUND CARD

A special card that turns your computer's bleeps and blurps into thundering booms and bangs. Besides improving sound quality, a sound card also lets you use speakers, a stereo, or a microphone with your computer.

SPEAKER

A device that produces sound and music when connected to a sound system. A sound system is only as good as its weakest link, so don't hook up a good sound card to the cheapest speakers you can find. For best results with multimedia, buy speakers with a built-in amplifier and accessible controls.

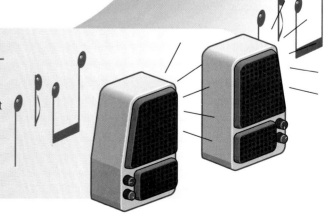

SPEECH RECOGNITION

Computer software that understands your voice, so you don't have to type. You can use speech recognition to dictate text for a document or to give commands to your computer. Speech recognition is extremely useful for people who are unable to type.

Dear Dr. Jones, Speech recognition allows me to dictate letters to my computer. But my co-workers think I'm talking to myself. They're spreading rumors. Do you think that I have a problem?

SPELL CHECK

A program available in most word processors that checks your spelling. The computer doesn't actually know how to spell — it simply compares every word in your document to words in its dictionary. If a word doesn't exist in the dictionary, the computer considers it misspelled.

SPLIT SCREEN

A screen you divide into sections in a spreadsheet program. This helps you view different areas of your document at the same time. For example, you can keep your spreadsheet headings on the screen while you scroll (move) through all your numbers.

Spooler – Storage Capacity

SPOOLER

See
PRINT BUFFER/
PRINT SPOOLER.

SRAM (STATIC RAM)

See CACHE (RAM).

SSL (SECURE SOCKETS LAYER)

See SECURITY (ONLINE).

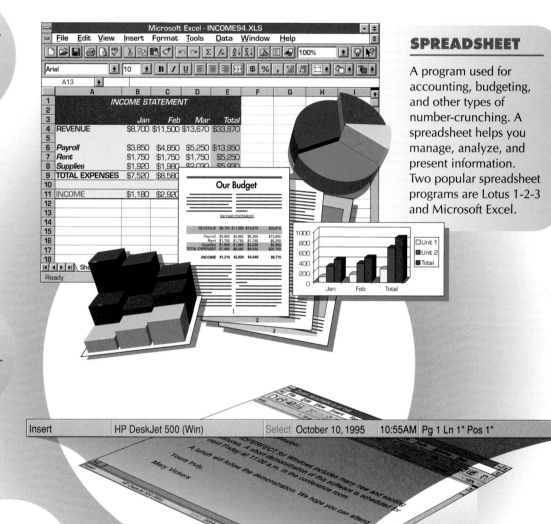

SPREADSHEET

A program used for accounting, budgeting, and other types of number-crunching. A spreadsheet helps you manage, analyze, and present information. Two popular spreadsheet programs are Lotus 1-2-3 and Microsoft Excel.

STATUS BAR

A strip along the bottom of the screen where most applications display information. It can include the current date and time, the position of the cursor on your screen, as well as other tidbits.

STATUS LIGHT

A little light on a computer case or peripheral. Most computers have status lights to indicate if the computer is on or a drive is being accessed. Modems have status lights to indicate the stage of a transmission (e.g., RD stands for Receiving Data).

STORAGE CAPACITY

How much information a floppy disk, hard disk, CD-ROM, or tape cartridge can hold. Storage capacity is given in kilobytes, megabytes, or gigabytes. You can never have too much storage capacity — just like you can never have too many closets at home. See also MEMORY CAPACITY.

STRIKEOUT/ STRIKETHROUGH

Text with a line through it. Editors often use strikeouts to indicate text they want to delete. Most word processors offer the strikeout option.

Strikeout

Document

60 point
Helvetica
Alignment - Left

11 point
Times New Roman
Alignment - Full

8 point
Futura
Alignment - Center

Style Sheet

Headline Style

Body Text Style

Caption Style

STYLE AND STYLE SHEET

On a page, headlines, body text, and captions can have different formatting characteristics (e.g., font size, font, alignment, etc.). Each set of formatting characteristics can be saved as a style. A style sheet contains all the styles (e.g., Headline, Body Text, Caption) used in a document.

In this example, the Headline style is 60 point, Helvetica, left-aligned. You can instantly format all the headlines in your document using this style. This saves time and improves the overall consistency of the document.

SUBDIRECTORY

A directory (folder) located inside another directory. Using subdirectories helps keep your computer system organized. For example, you can create a DATA directory on your hard drive and then make subdirectories inside it called EXLDATA and WPDATA. See also DIRECTORY.

SUBNOTEBOOK

A type of portable computer that weighs between two and six pounds. Subnotebooks are ideal for frequent travelers because of their light weight. This type of portable has less power, less storage space, and smaller screens than notebooks. See also NOTEBOOK COMPUTER.

SUBSCRIPT

A character that sits lower than the other characters on a line, like the "2" in H_2O.

SUITE

See SOFTWARE SUITE.

SUPERSCRIPT

A character that rises above the others in a line, like the "rd" in 3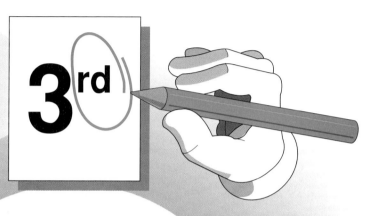rd.

SURGE PROTECTOR

A device that protects a computer from fluctuations in power. A surge protector regulates the amount of electricity that flows to the computer and prevents high-voltage surges from damaging a computer.

SVGA (SUPER VIDEO GRAPHICS ARRAY)

A video display standard for color monitors. SVGA monitors can display up to 16.7 million colors and resolutions up to 1,280 x 1,024 pixels. Most new computers offer SVGA. See also COLOR DEPTH, RESOLUTION (MONITOR), and VGA.

SWEDISH LOW-EMISSION STANDARDS

See MPR II.

SYMBOL FONT

A collection of Greek and other special characters that you can insert into your document. The symbol font can be used to represent mathematical symbols. This is one of the standard fonts included with Windows.

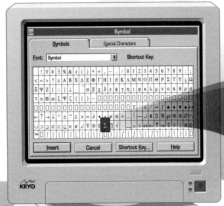

SYQUEST DRIVE

See REMOVABLE HARD DISK.

SYSTEM ADMINISTRATOR

See NETWORK ADMINISTRATOR.

SYSTEM TIME

The time according to the clock inside your computer. The clock runs even when the power is turned off. You have to adjust the time at least twice a year for Daylight Savings, because your computer is not quite that smart.

TABLE

Information organized in rows and columns. You can create tables with word processing, desktop publishing, spreadsheet, and database programs. A table can help you present related numbers or facts in an organized way.

EXPENSES

Category	1991	1992
Rent	$ 600.00	$ 684.00
Supplies	$ 342.00	$ 368.00
Advertising	$ 762.00	$ 650.00

TABLE

TABS

Settings that are used to line up columns of text in a document. Tabs are found on the ruler in most word processors.

In this example, spaces were used to line up the columns.

Last Name	First Name	Address	City	State	Zip Code
Appleton	Jill	456 John Street	Portland	OR	97526
DeVries	Monica	12 Willow Avenue	Los Angeles	CA	90032
Grossi	Rob	23 Riverbead Road	Seattle	WA	98109
Knill	Mark	97 Speers Road	Denver	CO	80207
	Justin	15 Lakeshore Drive	Atlanta	GA	30367
	Jennifer	34 Kerr Street	Provo	UT	84604
		56 Devon Road	Dallas	TX	75236

In this example, tabs were used to line up the columns.

Last Name	First Name	Address	City	State	Zip Code
Appleton	Jill	456 John Street	Portland	OR	97526
DeVries	Monica	12 Willow Avenue	Los Angeles	CA	90032
Grossi	Rob	23 Riverbead Road	Seattle	WA	98109
Knill	Mark	97 Speers Road	Denver	CO	80207
Leung	Justin	15 Lakeshore Drive	Atlanta	GA	30367
Matwey	Jennifer	34 Kerr Street	Provo	UT	84604
Smith	Albert	56 Devon Road	Dallas	TX	75236
Smith	Betty	111 Linton Street	Los Angeles	CA	90071
Smith	Carol	36 Ford Drive	Santa Clara	CA	95054
Anderson	David	55 Kennedy Road	Buffalo	NY	14213

TAPE DRIVE

See DAT DRIVE and QIC DRIVE.

TASKBAR

A strip along the bottom of your screen in Windows 95. The Taskbar displays the names of all your open windows. This lets you quickly switch between windows.

TCP/IP (TRANSMISSION CONTROL PROTOCOL/INTERNET PROTOCOL)

A common language that computers on the Internet use to communicate. Any computer that understands TCP/IP can connect to the Internet.

Information sent on the Internet is split up into "packets" about one page long. For example, to send a four-page report, your computer uses TCP/IP to split the report into four packets, address each one, and send each packet across the Internet.

Each packet makes several "hops" between computers, and likely takes a different route. When all four packets arrive, the destination computer uses TCP/IP to put them back together in the proper order.

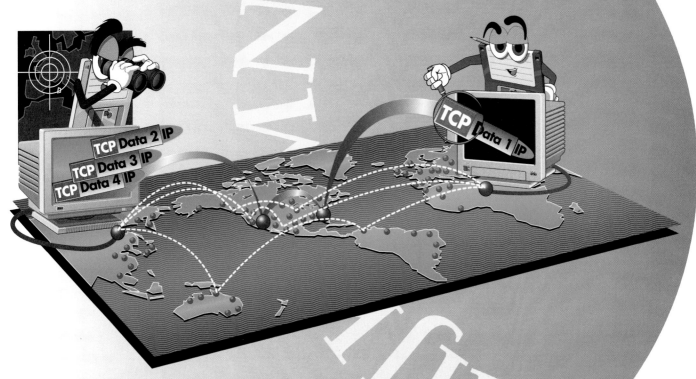

TCP (TRANSMISSION CONTROL PROTOCOL)

Divides a message into packets and then reassembles the packets when they all arrive at the destination. TCP also checks that the packets of a message arrived error-free.

IP (INTERNET PROTOCOL)

Defines how each packet of a message travels across the Internet. IP assigns an address to each packet. The computers on the Internet use the address to decide the best route for the packet.

TECHNICAL SUPPORT

The help desk or "hotline" provided by a hardware or software company to answer questions from customers. Most software, hardware, and mail order companies offer free technical support for a limited period of time. After that, you may have to pay — sort of like a psychiatrist who offers the first couple of sessions free.

TELECOMMUNICATIONS

The process of sending and receiving information over a distance, most often through a telephone system. To send and receive information with your computer, you need a modem, phone line, and telecommunications software.

TELNET

A program you can use to log onto another computer (host) on the Internet. You can then run programs and search databases on the remote computer as if you were actually sitting in front of that computer, instead of miles away in a different city or even a different country. You can use Telnet to access computerized libraries all over the world.

TEMPLATE

A document that provides the basic framework for a commonly used document in a word processing, spreadsheet, or desktop publishing program. You just fill in the blanks and the template takes care of the rest. Common templates include a fax cover sheet, an invoice, and a business letter.

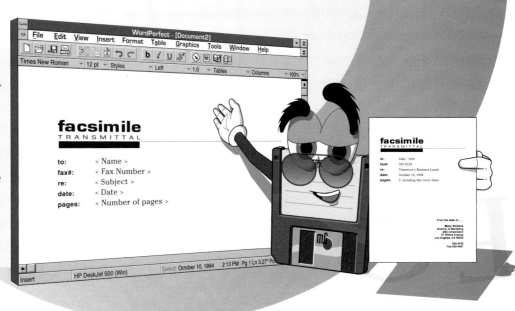

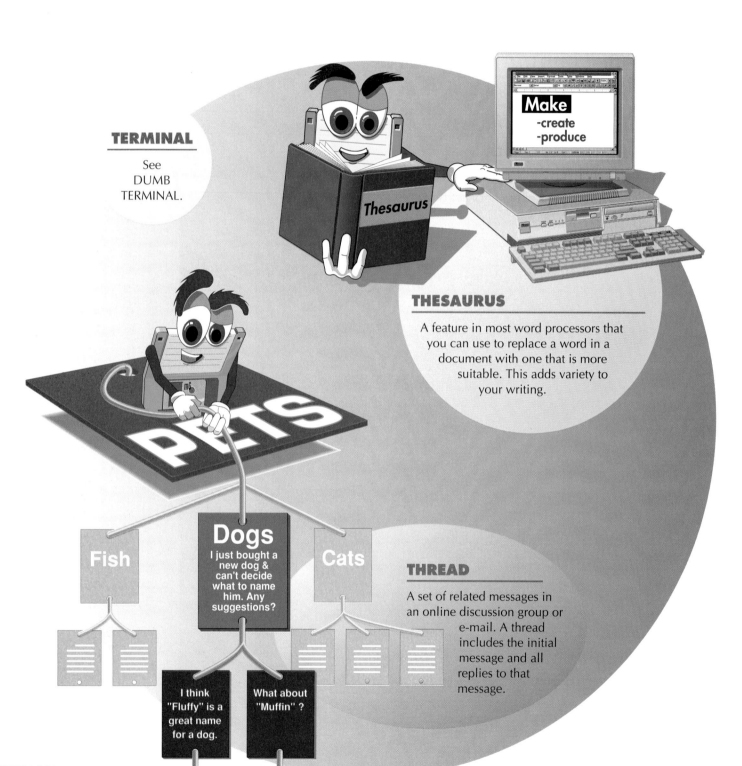

TERMINAL

See
DUMB
TERMINAL.

Make
-create
-produce

THESAURUS

A feature in most word processors that
you can use to replace a word in a
document with one that is more
suitable. This adds variety to
your writing.

Thesaurus

PETS

Fish

Dogs
I just bought a
new dog &
can't decide
what to name
him. Any
suggestions?

Cats

THREAD

A set of related messages in
an online discussion group or
e-mail. A thread
includes the initial
message and all
replies to that
message.

I think
"Fluffy" is a
great name
for a dog.

What about
"Muffin" ?

TILE

A way to arrange several windows on your screen so you can see the contents of each window. You can use tiling to place all your windows side by side, without overlapping them — kind of like shower tiles. See also CASCADE.

TILT AND SWIVEL STAND

A stand for your monitor that lets you move it in any direction. This lets you adjust your screen to the most comfortable position. Many monitors include built-in tilt and swivel stands.

TITLE BAR

A horizontal strip at the top of a window that displays the name of the program and document you are using. If the window is active, the title bar is highlighted.

Token-Ring Network – Traffic

TOKEN-RING NETWORK

A popular way to exchange information between computers on a network.

Token-ring works by passing a single token from computer to computer, around the network. To send a file, a computer must wait for the token to reach it, attach the file to the token, and then return both the token and the file to the network.

Everyone can use peripherals, such as a printer, on the network. To print a file, a computer attaches the file to the token and sends both the token and the attached file across the network to the printer.

When the token reaches the intended destination, the receiving computer or peripheral removes the file from the token. The token is then returned to the network so the process can start again.

TOOLBAR

A horizontal strip of buttons near the top of a window that provides shortcuts for commonly used commands. Some programs let you hide or display the toolbar, and even mix and match buttons to create a personal toolbar. Also called a button bar.

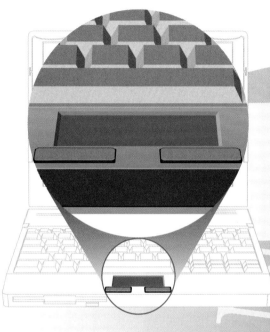

TOUCHPAD

A small pressure- and motion-sensitive area on a portable computer that you can use to move the mouse pointer. When you move your finger across the pad, the mouse pointer on the screen moves in the same direction. A touchpad is an alternative to a mouse.

TOWER CASE

See CASE.

TRACKBALL

An upside-down mouse that remains stationary on a portable computer. When you roll the trackball with your fingers or palm, the mouse pointer on the screen moves in the same direction. A trackball is an alternative to a mouse.

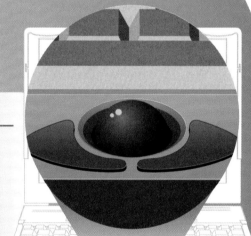

TRAFFIC

The volume of information carried over a computer network. Just like a highway, the more traffic on the network, the longer it takes to get through. When the traffic flow gets too heavy, the network administrator should look at enlarging the network to carry more traffic. See also BANDWIDTH.

TREE

The organization of files and directories (folders) on your hard drive. The main directory is called the "root directory." All the other directories are organized like the branches of an upside-down tree.
See also DIRECTORY and ROOT DIRECTORY.

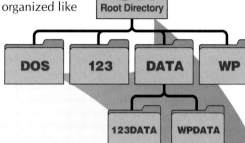

TRUE COLOR

Color that looks realistic in a video or photograph on your screen. True color is another name for 24-bit color or 16.7 million colors. True color is used mainly by professional designers and computer artists for retouching digital photos.

TRUETYPE

A font that looks the same on the screen as it does on a printout, even if you change the size of the text. TrueType lets you print high-quality fonts without an expensive printer, making it ideal for home and office use.

TRUETYPE
Font

TUTORIAL

A step-by-step lesson that explains how to perform tasks. Tutorials are available on paper, audio cassettes, or video. Some tutorials are built into the software as computer-based training or as a multimedia show-and-tell. See also CBT.

TYPE SIZE

The size of the characters in your document, given in points. There are approximately 72 points to an inch. Most business documents use 10 or 12 point type. You can change the type size to make text easier to read. Some examples of type sizes are:

5 point
10 point
15 point
20 point
25 point

TYPE STYLE

The appearance of the characters in your document. You can change the type style to emphasize important information. Some examples of type styles are:

Bold	Outline
Italic	~~Strikeout~~
<u>Underline</u>	Text^{Superscript}
Shadow	Text$_{Subscript}$

TYPEFACE

The design of the characters in your document. You can change the typeface to change the look of your document.

Some popular typefaces are:

Avant Garde

Bodoni

Courier

Helvetica

Optima

Times New Roman

UNDELETE

See
RECOVER.

UNDO

To reverse the last thing you did, sort of like taking back something you said but didn't mean. So if you just deleted a whole paragraph of text by mistake, you can use the Undo command to bring it back.

UNIX

A powerful operating system used in high-end workstations and computer systems on the Internet. It allows a single computer to operate multiple programs and be accessed by other computers, all at the same time.

UPGRADE OR UPGRADE KIT

To improve your PC by adding new features. Common hardware upgrades include adding more memory, a faster modem, or a larger monitor. You can upgrade your software by buying the latest version. Multimedia upgrade kits include a CD-ROM drive, sound card, and speakers.

UPLOAD

To send a file to another computer, such as a bulletin board system, an information service like CompuServe, or the Internet. Upload is the opposite of download.

UPS (UNINTERRUPTIBLE POWER SUPPLY)

A backup power supply for your computer. A UPS contains a battery that stores power. If the power fails, the UPS runs your computer long enough so you can save your work and shut down your computer. When the power returns, the battery in your UPS is recharged.

URL (UNIFORM RESOURCE LOCATOR)

The address, or location, of a document on the World Wide Web. Like a home address, each document has a unique URL. See also WORLD WIDE WEB.

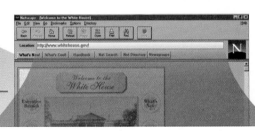

http://www.whitehouse.gov/

USENET

Part of the Internet that consists of thousands of discussion groups, called newsgroups. Usenet allows individuals with common interests to communicate with one another. See also NEWSGROUP.

VAPORWARE

Software that has been announced by a
manufacturer but not released. Most delays
are caused by the sheer complexity of creating
a stable and bug-free product. Never depend
on vaporware — software isn't software until
you have it in your hands.

VERONICA

A search tool on the Internet
that helps you find documents
of interest. Veronica uses the
word you specify to search
Gopher menus around the
world. See also GOPHER.

VERSION NUMBER

The number before the decimal place in a
program's number. A different version number
indicates major improvements to the software.
For example, Excel 5.0 for Windows included
many additional features and user-friendly
enhancements to Excel 4.0 for Windows.
See also RELEASE NUMBER.

VGA (VIDEO GRAPHICS ARRAY)

A video display standard for color monitors. VGA monitors display 16 colors at a resolution of 640 x 480 pixels. This is the minimum standard for computer systems. VGA is not recommended for multimedia applications. See also COLOR DEPTH, RESOLUTION (MONITOR), and SVGA.

VIDEO ADAPTER

An expansion card that controls the images displayed on your screen. Your video adapter determines the monitor's color depth and resolution. The most popular video adapters support SVGA. See also COLOR DEPTH, RESOLUTION (MONITOR), and SVGA.

VIRTUAL MEMORY

A way of using part of the hard disk to simulate more memory (RAM) than actually exists. This allows a computer to run more programs at the same time. Virtual memory is slower than RAM — that's why adding more RAM speeds up the computer. See also RAM.

Virtual Reality – VRML

VIRTUAL REALITY (VR)

A computer-generated, 3-D, imaginary world. Special VR software allows you to enter and interact with images in this artificial world. Different levels of virtual reality exist, from partial to total immersion.

PARTIAL IMMERSION

In this form of VR, you use your keyboard and mouse to interact with an imaginary world. You view this world through the eyes of a fictional character, usually the hero or heroine. On-screen graphics change as you navigate through this artificial space. Two examples are Id Software's DOOM action game and LucasArts' Dark Forces.

TOTAL IMMERSION

In this form of VR, you are totally immersed and interacting in a 3-D, imaginary world. This can be accomplished by wearing oversized goggles and a special glove wired to the computer. By moving your head and hand, you tell the computer how to navigate through the virtual world. This type of VR is used in medicine, the military, and for entertainment.

VIRUS

A program that disrupts the normal operation of a computer. It can cause a variety of problems, from the appearance of annoying messages to the destruction of information on your hard drive.

Viruses can infect your computer from incoming modem transmissions. They can also enter your computer through an infected floppy disk or through a network connection. See also ANTI-VIRUS SOFTWARE.

VL-BUS OR VESA BUS

The electronic path (or bus) between a computer's CPU (or brain) and monitor. The VL-Bus is primarily used with 486 computers to speed up the display of graphics on the screen. It is much faster than the ISA bus. See also CPU and ISA BUS.

VRAM (VIDEO RANDOM ACCESS MEMORY)

A type of memory used in video adapters to create images on your screen. High-end applications such as desktop publishing and photo-retouching use VRAM. Low-end, general-purpose video adapters use DRAM. VRAM is faster, but more expensive, than DRAM. See also DRAM.

VRML (VIRTUAL REALITY MODELING LANGUAGE)

A way to create virtual realities (imaginary worlds) that people can access over the Internet. You can enter and move through virtual museums, libraries, and spaceships. VRML lets you jump from one virtual place to another. See also VIRTUAL REALITY.

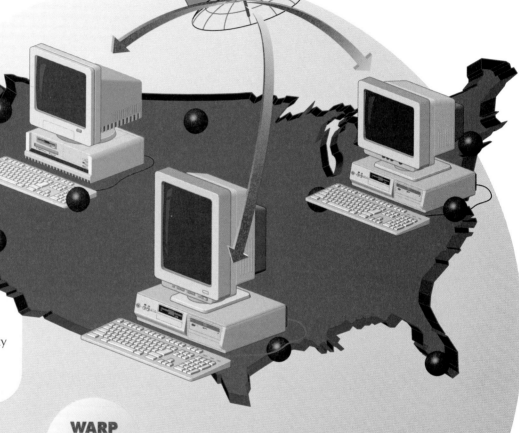

WAN (WIDE AREA NETWORK)

Several PCs connected together so they can share files and computer equipment, as well as exchange e-mail. A wide area network connects computers across a large geographic area, such as a city or country. The Internet is an example of a WAN. See also LAN.

WARP

See OS/2 WARP.

WAVETABLE SYNTHESIS

The way that better sound cards produce sound. Wavetable synthesis creates realistic, high-quality sound by using actual recordings of musical instruments. Sound cards that use wavetable synthesis are more expensive, but sound better than cards that use FM synthesis. See also FM SYNTHESIS.

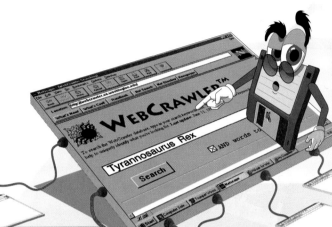

WEBCRAWLER

A search tool you can use to find information on the World Wide Web. Webcrawler is a free service on the Internet. To use Webcrawler, point your Web browser to http://www.webcrawler.com. Webcrawler is an alternative to Lycos and Yahoo. See also LYCOS, WORLD WIDE WEB, and YAHOO.

WILDCARD

A special symbol that represents one or more characters. Wildcards are useful when you want to find a file and only know part of its name.

The two most common wildcards are the asterisk (*) and the question mark (?). The question mark represents a single character in a file name. The asterisk represents one or more characters in a file name.

WILDCARD	FINDS
Letter?.doc	Letter1.doc Letter2.doc, etc...
*.doc	all files ending in doc
Letter.*	all files starting with Letter
.	all files

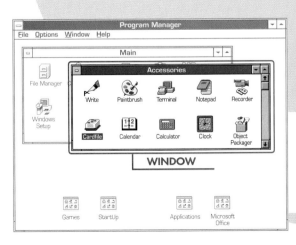

WINDOW

WINDOW

A rectangle on your screen that displays information. A window can contain little pictures (icons), a document, or an application.

Windows 3.1

WINDOWS 3.1

A program that works with MS-DOS to control the overall activity of your computer.

THE WINDOWS 3.1 SCREEN

The **Program Manager** is the control center where you start programs.

A **window** is a rectangle on your screen that displays information.

A **group icon** contains similar program icons. For example, the Games group icon contains several games.

Note: An icon is a small picture on your screen that represents an object, such as a file or program.

A **program icon** lets you start a program. Programs allow you to write letters, analyze numbers, create presentations and much more.

A mouse is essential when working with Windows.

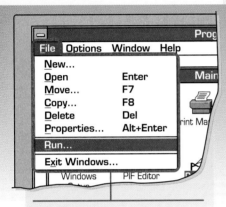

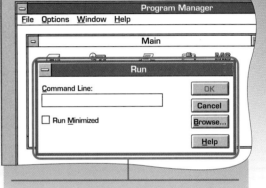

In Windows 3.1, you select commands from menus to accomplish tasks. For example, the Run command lets you start a program or open a document.

When you select a command, a dialog box may appear. It lets you select options before carrying out a command. For example, the Run dialog box lets you choose the program or document you want to open.

Windows 3.1 lets you run several programs at the same time. This lets you instantly switch between programs. For example, you can write a letter and then instantly switch to another program to check your sales figures.

• Most Windows programs look and act the same. Once you learn one program, you can quickly learn others.

• You can easily exchange information between programs.

Windows 3.1 – Windows NT

WINDOWS 3.1

The **File Manager** is a program in Windows 3.1 that lets you view and organize all the files stored on your computer. You can use the File Manager to sort, copy, move, and delete files.

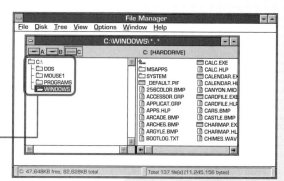

Windows 3.1 uses directories (folders) to help organize the information stored on your computer.

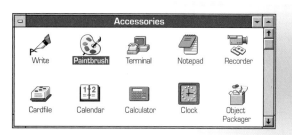

Windows 3.1 provides several **accessories**, or mini-programs, that help you accomplish simple tasks. For example, the Paintbrush program lets you draw pictures, maps, and signs.

The **Control Panel** lets you change the way Windows 3.1 looks and acts. You can change the date set in the computer, the colors displayed on the screen, and much more.

WINDOWS FOR WORKGROUPS 3.11

A more powerful version of Windows 3.1. This program looks and acts like Windows 3.1 but operates faster, includes a few new applications, and lets you exchange information through a network.

WINDOWS NT

Stands for Windows New Technology (NT). A program that targets the top 10 percent of computer users who need a powerful operating system. Unlike Windows 3.1 and Windows for Workgroups 3.11, this program is a true operating system because it does not need MS-DOS to operate.

Windows NT lets you exchange information through a network. It also provides security features to protect information and lets you use up to 255 characters to name a document.

WINDOWS 95

A program that controls the overall activity of your computer. It is the successor of Windows 3.1.

THE WINDOWS 95 SCREEN

My Computer lets you view all the folders and documents stored on your computer.

The **Recycle Bin** stores all the documents you delete and allows you to recover them later.

The **Start Button** gives you quick access to programs and documents.

You can place a **shortcut** to a document on your screen. This lets you quickly open documents you use regularly.

The **Taskbar** displays the name of each open window on your screen. This lets you easily switch between the open windows.

Windows 95 is more graphical than Windows 3.1 and easier to use.

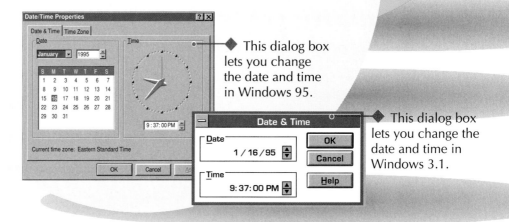

◆ This dialog box lets you change the date and time in Windows 95.

◆ This dialog box lets you change the date and time in Windows 3.1.

Windows 95 supports Plug and Play technology. This technology lets you add new features to a computer without complex and time-consuming installation procedures.

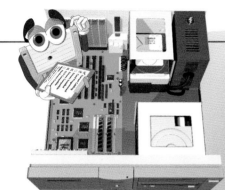

Windows 95 lets you use up to 255 characters to name a document.

Note: Windows 3.1 filenames can be up to 8 characters long with a 3 character extension (example: myletter.doc).

Windows 95 comes with a program called Windows Explorer that lets you view the location of each folder and document on your computer. You can use the Explorer to manage your information.

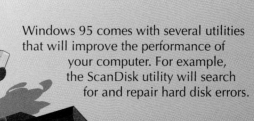

Windows 95 comes with several utilities that will improve the performance of your computer. For example, the ScanDisk utility will search for and repair hard disk errors.

Wizard - WYSIWYG

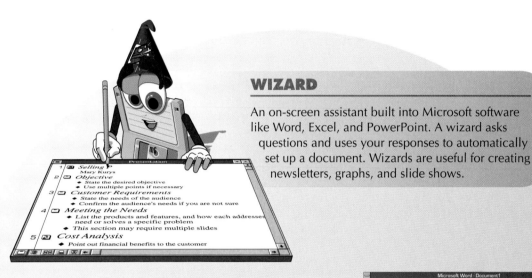

WIZARD

An on-screen assistant built into Microsoft software like Word, Excel, and PowerPoint. A wizard asks questions and uses your responses to automatically set up a document. Wizards are useful for creating newsletters, graphs, and slide shows.

WORD PROCESSOR

Software you can use to produce documents, including letters, reports, manuals, and newsletters. Most word processors include a built-in spell check and thesaurus to increase the accuracy and quality of a document. Two popular word processors are WordPerfect and Word.

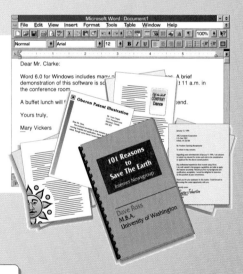

WORD WRAP

A feature in most word processors that automatically moves words to the next line as you type. You only have to press the Enter key when you want to leave a blank line or start a new paragraph.

When using a word processor to type a letter, the text au...

When using a word processor to type a letter, the text automatically wraps to the next line as you type.

WORKS PROGRAMS

See INTEGRATED SOFTWARE.

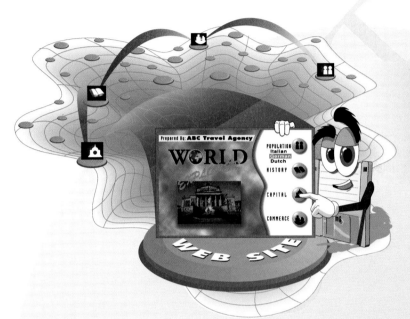

WORLD WIDE WEB (WWW)

The fastest-growing and most user-friendly section of the Internet that lets you access text, graphics, sound, and even video. Many groups, companies, and individuals provide "pages" of free information on the WWW.

Not Write-Protected

Write-Protected

WRITE-PROTECTED

Protection against erasing and recording information on a floppy disk. You can write-protect a 3.5 inch floppy disk by moving a little plastic tab to the write-protected position.

WYSIWYG

WYSIWYG stands for "What You See Is What You Get" and is pronounced "wizzy wig." WYSIWYG simply means the text and graphics displayed on your screen exactly match your printouts.

X-AXIS

See AXIS.

XMODEM PROTOCOL

A language used by modems. Xmodem ensures that a file is transmitted correctly, but it is slow and inefficient. For example, if a transmission is interrupted, Xmodem has to resend the entire file. Xmodem is gradually being replaced by Zmodem, a newer protocol. See also PROTOCOL and ZMODEM PROTOCOL.

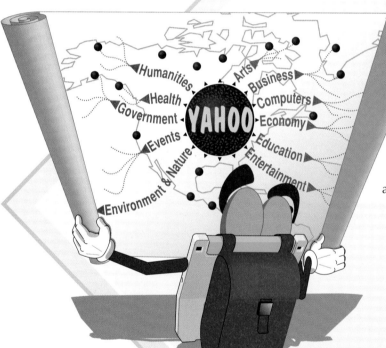

YAHOO

One of the most popular search tools to find "pages" on the World Wide Web. Yahoo is organized by subjects, such as Art, Business, Computers, Economy, and even What's Cool? To use Yahoo, point your Web browser to http://www.yahoo.com. See also BROWSER and WORLD WIDE WEB.

Y-AXIS

See AXIS.

ZIF SOCKET

A socket that enables you to easily remove and replace a CPU chip to upgrade your computer. You use a tiny handle to release the old chip and clamp down the new one. ZIF stands for Zero Insertion Force. See also CPU.

Z-AXIS

See AXIS.

XYZ

ZIPPED FILE

A file that has been squeezed down using PKZIP compression software. Files that are compressed travel faster between modems. To return the file to its original size, PKUNZIP decompression software is used. See also COMPRESSION.

ZMODEM PROTOCOL

A language used by modems. Zmodem ensures that a file is transmitted correctly. Zmodem is faster and more efficient than Xmodem, because if a transmission is interrupted, Zmodem doesn't have to resend the entire file. Instead, it continues where it left off. See also PROTOCOL and XMODEM PROTOCOL.

ZONE

The last part of an Internet address, which indicates the type of organization. See also INTERNET ADDRESS.

ZONE	MEANING
COM	commercial
EDU	educational
GOV	government
NET	network
ORG	miscellaneous organization

ZOOM

To enlarge or reduce the display of text or graphics on your screen. For example, you can zoom in to read small text or zoom out to view all the text on a page.

Acronyms

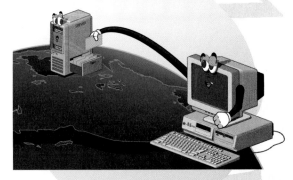

Acronyms

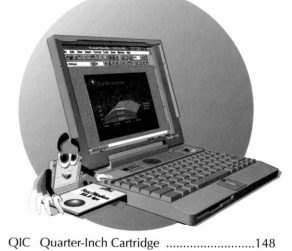

http://www.whitehouse.gov/

Internet Terms

Internet Terms

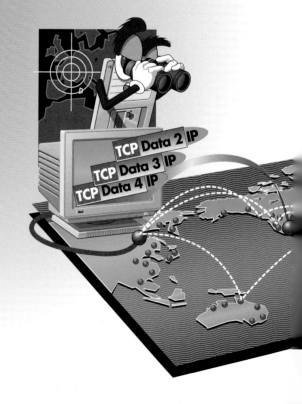

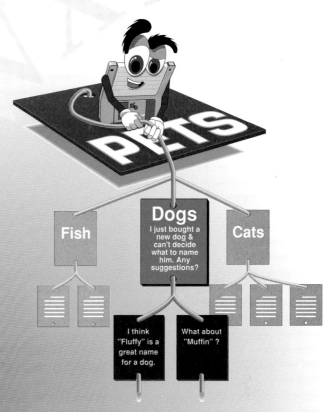

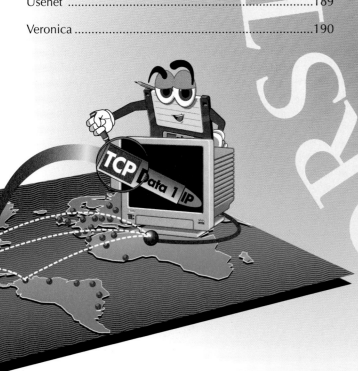